The
Of ART
𝕾𝖕𝖎𝖗𝖎𝖙𝖚𝖆𝖑 𝖂𝖆𝖗𝖋𝖆𝖗𝖊

*Strategies for
Effective
Spiritual Warfare*

Includes a comparative study of the teachings of
Military Strategist, Sun Tzu & *"The Art of War"*

Dr. Jacquelyn Hadnot

The Art of Spiritual Warfare

Reviews

War is no respecter of persons and Dr. Jacquie teaches us how war has a destructive nature. War means fighting, but in the Kingdom of God, we are to fight the good fight of faith. *The Art of Spiritual Warfare* has made an impact in my life. It has allowed me to understand the nature of spiritual warfare. Being in a war can be very complex if you do not understand who and what you are fighting. This book has illuminated warfare strategies, tactics and combative techniques. This book will be a blessing to anyone in the midst of warfare. Remember, you are in the army now!

Minister Dale Fountain, Overland Park KS

Dr. Jacquie's, *The Art of Spiritual Warfare*, is a great book to have in your arsenal of weaponry because it will prepare you for spiritual warfare. You can apply the teachings in this book to your life's principles as tools and strategies for effective spiritual warfare. It also breaks down the methods of Satan as well as his kingdom and hierarchy in ways everyone can comprehend.

Evangelist Lateresa Williams, Little Rock AR

I am very proud of the gift that God has placed in this mighty woman of God. She has studied and taught the essence of spiritual warfare, and written a tool, *The Art of Spiritual Warfare*, that disarms the enemy and his plans against Christianity in this century. Dr Jacquie Hadnot is a tremendous blessing to the body of Christ and a true soldier to the body of Christ according to Ephesians 6. This book will be a blessing to anyone seeking insight into kingdom warfare.

Pastor Leland Thomas, Kansas City MO

The Art of Spiritual Warfare

The Art of Spiritual Warfare: Strategies for Effective Spiritual Warfare
Dr. Jacquelyn Hadnot
Published by: Igniting the Fire Publishing
1314 North 38th Street
Kansas City, KS 66102
www.ignitingthefire.net

No part of this publication may be reproduced, stored in a retrieval system, or transmitted, in any form or by any means, electronic, mechanical, photocopying, recording, or otherwise, without the written prior permission of the author.

Unless otherwise noted, all Scripture quotations are taken from King James Version of the Bible.

Scripture quotations marked AMP are taken from The Amplified Bible AMP. The Amplified Bible, Old Testament copyright © 1965, 1987 by the Zondervan Corporation. The Amplified New Testament, copyright © 1954, 1958, 1987 by the Lockman Foundation. Used by permission.

Scripture quotations marked NASB are taken from The New American Standard Bible AMP. Copyright © 1960, 1962, 1963, 1968, 1971, 1972, 1973, 1975, 1977 by the Zondervan Corporation. The Amplified New Testament, copyright © 1954, 1958, 1987 by the Lockman Foundation. Used by permission.

Scripture quotations marked NIV are taken from The New International Version. Copyright © 1973, 1978, 1984 by the International Bible Society. Used by permission.

Cover Design: Dr. Jacquelyn Hadnot
Copyright© 2012 by Dr. Jacquelyn Hadnot
All rights reserved.

Please note that Igniting the Fire's publishing style capitalizes certain pronouns in Scripture that refer to the Father, Son, and Holy Spirit, and may differ from some Bible publishers' styles.

ISBN 0615596541

Dedication

This book is dedicated to the Kingdom Cops that are holding down the kingdom block.

Prepare for War!

Acknowledgements

To my Lord and Savior, Jesus Christ: Thank You for loving and trusting me to carry Your word. The more I am in Your presence the more I desire to sit at Your feet. You are my greatest inspiration.

To the family that loves, supports and enriches my life:

- My husband, Minister Gregory Hadnot for taking the time to hear God's heart through me.
- My daughter, Jacquanda, you are the joy of my heart.
- My grandson, Tristan I love you, can we go outside?
- My brother and friend, Pastor Leland Thomas, International Prayer Intercessor.
- Vincent and Barbara Jarrett, you are the best.
- Priest Eleazar, you have taught me so much about blending the fragrant anointing oils that bless the Kingdom of God.
- Pastor Valarie Thornton, you are such an awesome woman of God, thanks for always being there.
- Apostle Sarah White, you are my [girl!] Woman of God words cannot express my heart for you.
- To the volunteers and family at It Is Written Ministries, I love you all so much.

Contents

Foreword	9
Introduction: It's Time to Arm Yourself!	11
1. You're in the Army Now!	17
2. What is War?	27
3. What is Spiritual Warfare?	31
4. A House Swept Clean	37
5. Armed & Ready	51
6. Meet the General	61
7. What Are You Fighting?	71
8. The Battlefield is YOUR MIND!	79
9. The Devices and Doctrines of Satan..............	87
10. Worldly Warfare vs. Spiritual Warfare..........	117
11. The Strategy of Warfare	123
12. Is Your House Clean?..................................	149
13. Launching a Counter Attack	157
14. Exposing Satan's Kingdom of Darkness	171
15. Destroying the Works of the Enemy	187
16. Closing Portals, Doors and Gateways	197
17. The Warfare of Prayer	207
18. The Importance of Prayer	213
19. The Enemy Hates Your Worship	219
20. Having Done All, To Stand	227
21. The Lord is Your Battle Ax	245
22. Declarative Prayers	255
Appendix	
Scriptures on Standing	293
Demon List: Strongmen & Their Subordinate Spirits	295
Twelve Spirits Raging Against the Church	309
About the Author	315
Books & Materials by Dr. Jacquie	317

The Art of Spiritual Warfare

Foreword

First, I would like to thank our Lord and Savior Jesus Christ for giving Apostle Jacquie Hadnot such boldness and love for God and for His people. Since I have known her, I found her to be faithful to the Lord, her family, and the ministry.

I have observed her increase in the revelation and knowledge of deliverance. I can honestly say that during the years that I have been a part of her ministry, she has never wavered in her commitment to the call on her life. She does not compromise nor is she afraid to preach or teach the truth. Her only concern is to see God's people set free and to see people with bruised and hurt lives delivered. She has helped many people throughout her years in ministry and this book contains some of their testimonies.

She has written several books and recorded numerous teachings and music CDs that have assisted people in breaking free from the bondages of the enemy. Her books include Cry Aloud, Spare Not, Closing the Doors to Satan's Attacks, the Enemy in Me, and several others.

Apostle Jacquie's ministry has been a blessing to my congregation and me. She has a special anointing in the ministry of prayer. God has endowed her with the wisdom to birth powerful warfare strategies to enlighten and equip the body of Christ. Often, the enemy's traps and snares bind people and they don't know how to break free.

Apostle Jacquie's book, *The Art of Spiritual Warfare,* exposes curses, the demonic spirits operating behind them and practical ways to bind the enemy and break his strongholds. This is a powerful book and it will open your eyes to the realm of spiritual warfare. *The Art of Spiritual Warfare* gives you practical and powerful strategies that will break demonic strongholds on your life, your finances, your family, etc.

Upon reading this book, the power of God will begin to set you free from the power of darkness. You will be set free from strongholds. *The Art of Spiritual Warfare* will also give you the power to cut the umbilical cord of ungodly soul ties and generational curses. It will remove the dark areas in your life so that God can use you in greater ways. After breaking the curses, she teaches you how to loose blessings over yourself and your family.

This book is not for the faint in heart, but for those who desire unbroken fellowship with God, those who desire more. It will teach you how to release the fire of the living God in your ministry and your life.

The Art of Spiritual Warfare is necessary for Christians looking for a training manual to guide you in understanding the war that is being waged against you.

Pastor Valerie Thornton
At His Feet Ministries

Introduction
It's Time to Arm Yourself!

Believers, this is the day for which you were born - for such a time as this. It is a day of freedom, a day of holy boldness, when you can come out of hiding from your enemy, take up your armor, and stand as the mighty warrior of God you were predestined to be.

It is a day when the church is being freed from tolerance, compromise, secular Christianity and arising to take its rightful place as a citadel for kingdom warriors. The church will become a mighty fortress that will train and equip kingdom people with a kingdom mindset. As you read this book, allow it to empower you for this new day. A day that cries, "We will not hold back, shut up or shut down. We will advance for the Kingdom of God."

This book was birthed after years of engaging spiritual warfare in my personal life, walking others through spiritual warfare and deliverance and teaching Christians how to war in the spirit.

I realized that people were living defeated lives due to the lack of training on spiritual warfare. They talked around it, laid out an apologetic explaining why believers could not firmly stand in the midst of adversity or worse quoted a myriad of clichés that had nothing to do with spiritual warfare.

E.M. Bounds wrote in his book, Guide to Spiritual Warfare, "Christians may live and die completely unaware of the devil's existence and hatred. At the same time, Satan is indifferent to their religion because they are not threatening his kingdom." It is vital that the church give precedence to the need for spiritual warfare if we are going to escape the spiritual beheading that

Introduction

Satan has planned for individuals who are not armed and prepared for the battle. It is mandatory that we understand spiritual warfare, if we are going to take territory and advance for the kingdom of God.

There have been many books written about spiritual warfare and I have listed some of them in the Recommended Reading section. I pray they will help you on your journey as a freedom fighter.

I taught a course on spiritual warfare and prayer. From that course, the Lord led me to write this book and write it in a way that individuals from all lifestyles and every area of ministry could grasp the necessity for spiritual warfare. I chose to write this book at a time when my health came under attack. I recall the warning I received from the enemy, he said, "If you leave the book alone your health will improve." One thing is for sure, Satan does not want his kingdom exposed and he is relentless when it comes to shutting you down. I chose to stand, endure the trial of my health and come out victorious for the glory of God. Satan could only buffet me through my health, he had no authority to take my life, therefore, I chose to stand and resist the demonic assaults that tried to stop this book.

As a child of the Most High, you must also stand in the midst of the battle, armed with the full armor of God, and stand unmovable and unshakable. We must stand like Shammah who was left alone in the middle of the field of beans after everyone had deserted him. Shammah stood ready to defend the field, confident that God would bring a great victory. He defended it, struck the Philistines down, and the Lord brought about a great victory (2 Samuel 23:11-12).

Scripture warns us to give no place [room] to him [Satan] to advance against us. "To keep Satan from getting the advantage over us; for we are not ignorant of his wiles and intentions and leave no [such] room or foothold for the devil [give no opportunity to him] (Second Corinthians 2:11; Ephesians 4:27 AMP, respectively).

The Art of Spiritual Warfare is designed to train and equip you as you move into the position, which God has called us, the position of kingdom warriors. As you journey through this book, I pray that your "spiritual antenna" will be in tune to the voice of the Lord and you will take a new posture in your warfare strategy. If you don't have a warfare strategy, I hope this book will encourage you to position yourself to become skilled at spiritual warfare strategies.

If you have found yourself defeated each time you engage a battle or worse running from a battle, today is the last day you will surrender ground to the enemy or be defeated. It is time for you to rise up and take your rightful place as a modern day Deborah, Barak, Gideon, Joshua, or Esther. It is time to rise up and access the authority given to us by Christ Jesus. Take up your sword and rise! You are about to discover *The Art of Spiritual Warfare*.

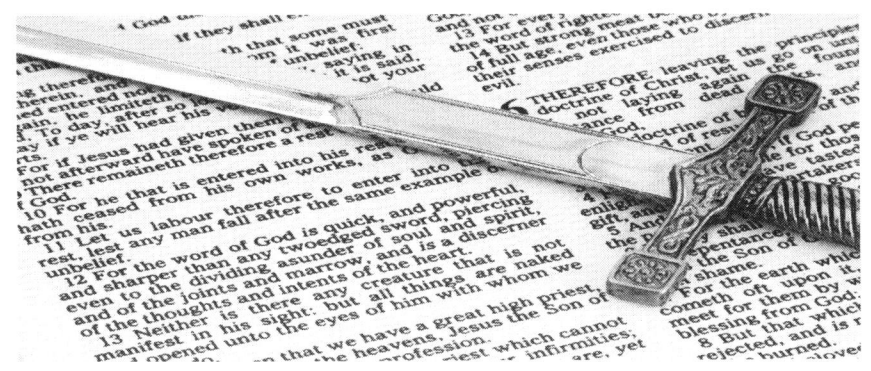

Chapter 1

You're In the Army Now!

"Praise be to the LORD my Rock, who trains my hands for war, my fingers for battle. He is my loving God and my fortress, my stronghold and my deliverer, my shield, in whom I take refuge, who subdues peoples under me" (Psalm 144:1-2). *"Though an army besiege me, my heart will not fear; though war break out against me, even then will I be confident"* (Psalm 27:3).

War is not an attractive subject, neither is it humane or selfless and it takes no prisoners. War is no respecter of persons. The essence of war is conquest and destruction. Your ability to engage the warfare will determine whether you are the victor or the victim. Because of the destructive nature of war, it is important that you have a warfare strategy if you are going to survive the battle and win the victory. Our spiritual inheritance is tied to our ability to stand in the midst of the war.

> *Our spiritual inheritance is tied to our ability to stand in the midst of the war.*

"The enemy boasted, 'I will pursue, I will overtake them. I will divide the spoils; I will gorge myself on them. I will draw my sword and my hand will destroy them.' But you blew with your breath, and the sea covered them. They sank like lead in the mighty waters" (Exodus 15:9-10).

"Therefore I will give him a portion among the great, and he will divide the spoils with the strong, because he poured out his life unto death, and was numbered with the transgressors. For he bore the sin of many, and made intercession for the transgressors" (Isaiah 53:12).

In warfare involving nations, the fight is usually over land, property or resources. Wars that are fought over resources such as oil or water are often fought from generation to generation. The same applies to wars that are fought over land possession. Extremist groups will fight to the death to secure a parcel of land. Wars are still fought today over land, oil, family or generational disputes. Suicide bombers determined to destroy their enemies will slaughter thousands in order to bring attention to their purpose. Children are recruited as suicide bombers with no thought to the future of the children, the people they hurt or the lives they destroy.

Jihads (Islamic campaign waged by Muslims in defense of the Islamic faith against people, organizations, or countries regarded as hostile to Islam) are declared that perpetuate death and destruction in order to bring their *"holy war"* to the forefront.

World leaders convene in war rooms (military operations center) strategizing the next battle plan for fighting on foreign soil, while at the same time disregarding the civil unrest that is at the doors of their own countries.

The United States has had civil wars or unrest in the past ranging from fighting over the abolition of slavery to riots on the streets of major cities. I believe that civil wars are far more dangerous and devastating than any world war. Why? Unlike wars fought between armed forces, civil war relates to what happens within a state or between different citizens or groups of citizens.

Examples:

- Citizens against the federal government
- Citizens against the city or state government
- Employees against employers
- Hispanics against deportation in America
- Klu Klux Klan against African Americans
- Anti-Semitics against Jewish citizens
- Abortionists against Anti-Abortionists

Spiritual warfare is similar in nature. In spiritual warfare, you will find:

- Satan against believers.
- Principalities against believers
- Powers against believers
- Rulers of the darkness against believers.
- Spiritual wickedness against believers.
- Spirit of anti-Christ against Christ, the church and believers.

"And it was given unto him to make war with the saints, and to overcome them: and power was given him over all kindreds, and tongues, and nations" (Revelation 13:7).

Spiritual warfare is fought on every level. No one can escape the fist of warfare. Some individuals believe we should not concern ourselves with the knowledge of demonic forces and spiritual warfare. Without knowledge of your enemy, you are headed for defeat and destruction. There are individuals who believe we are powerless against Satan and his demonic strategies. We are neither powerless nor helpless, but in order to survive, we must know our real enemy and possess a sound knowledge of our spiritual artillery. We must be fully equipped to fight against our greatest adversary, the kingdom of darkness. You must have knowledge of the demonic forces fighting against you. You must:

- Recognize your enemy.
- Expose Satan's kingdom of darkness.
- Destroy the works of your enemy.
- Brings other individuals out of darkness.
- Give God glory for the victory.

"For we wrestle not against flesh and blood, but against principalities, against powers, against the rulers of the darkness of this world, against spiritual wickedness in high places" (Ephesians 6:12).

This book is your *"Art of War"* instruction manual for effective spiritual warfare. Soldiers must be properly trained before they are sent to the battlefield. Without proper training, the enemy will take you out before you have a chance to draw your weapon. Like all instruction manuals, you will be taught the fundamental elements of warfare.

- The weapons of your warfare.
- How to recognize your enemy.
- Exposing Satan's devices and doctrines.
- Steps to defeat Satan's strategies.
- Strategies based on strategist, General Sun Tzu.
- Declarative warfare prayers.

People have said that they were afraid to pray for or touch individuals they praying for because they did not want demons to transfer. FEAR NOT! We have authority over the realm of Satan. Instead of being afraid of demons, know that demons are afraid of us because we are children of the Most High God. James 2:19 assures us that demons tremble and believe in God. The Greek translation for the word "flee" means to run from someone or something. When we call on the name of Jesus, the demons tremble. Therefore, access the authority you have been given by our Lord, Jesus Christ, stand on the Word of God and FEAR NOT because "at the name of Jesus every knee should bow, in heaven and on earth and under the earth, and every tongue confess that Jesus Christ is Lord, to the glory of God the Father" (Philippians 2:10-11).

You are in the army now! It is time to lock, load, and dig in for the battle.

The Art of Spiritual Warfare

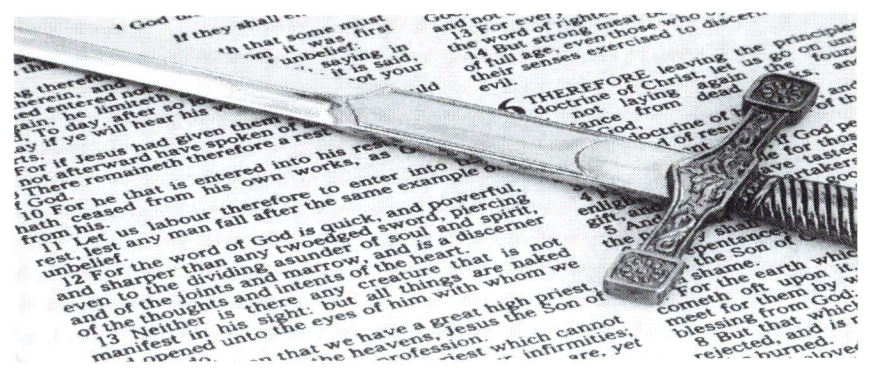

Chapter 2

What is War?

"A wise man has great power, and a man of knowledge increases strength; for waging war you need guidance, and for victory many advisers."

(Proverbs 24:5-6)

War is defined as:

1. **Armed fighting between groups:** a period of

hostile relations between countries, states, or factions that leads to fighting between armed forces, especially in land, air, or sea battles.
2. **Methods of warfare:** the techniques or the study of the techniques of armed conflict.
3. A serious struggle, argument, or conflict between people.
4. An effort to combat or eradicate something harmful.

We are in a war and the war is against the kingdom of darkness. It is a war that is not fought in the flesh, but a war that is fought in the spiritual realm. We are fighting against an enemy that we cannot see with the natural eye. An enemy that is so clever and deceptive that he will not stop in his quest to destroy us. He is clever and deceptive because he has had thousands of years to study us and he knows how we function. Satan does not have original thoughts or plans; instead, he uses tricks and deceptions to come against us. If we are not aware of his tricks and devices, he has a legal right to walk in through the front door and wage war. If we do not watch and pray, he will try to take us out. We are not fighting an enemy that plays fair; he knows every dirty trick in the book because he wrote the book. He came to steal, kill and destroy every area of your life.

As soldiers on the battlefield, we must stand in the midst of the battle, confident in Christ that we are already victorious because our Commander in Chief has already devised the battle plan; our responsibility is to follow the plan with obedience and confidence.

Now that you have an understanding of war, it is now time to address spiritual warfare.

The Art of Spiritual Warfare

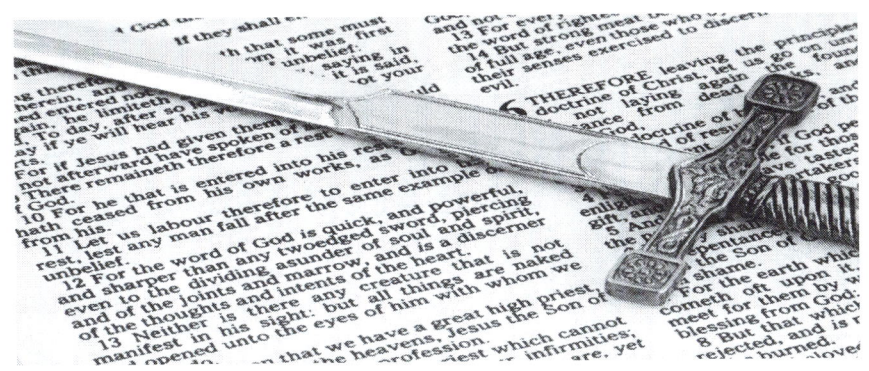

Chapter 3
What is Spiritual Warfare?

Spiritual Warfare is waging war in the spirit realm. A battle or attack that comes from the invisible spheres of the heavenly realm. *Spiritual Warfare* is a covert war. Covert means secret, concealed, out of sight, clandestine war. Because spiritual warfare is invisible, many believers do not realize they are engaged in battle until they have suffered a defeat or deadly assault. Spiritual warfare has two objectives: to bring destruction to the Kingdom of God and bring glory to the kingdom of Satan. Through demonic warfare tactics, the enemy can manipulate any situation, defeat you and leave you bloody and battered on the battlefield.

Dr. C. Peter Wagner, in his book, *Warfare Prayers*, suggests three general levels of warfare:

1. **Ground level spiritual warfare**…as when Jesus gave his disciples "power over unclean spirits, to cast them out..." (Matthew 10:1 NKJ).
2. **Occult level spiritual warfare**…involving demonic power at work through shamans, New Age channelers, occult practitioners, witches, and warlocks, Satanist priests, fortune-tellers, and the like…(Paul's experience in Philippi - Acts 16:16-24).
3. **Strategic level spiritual warfare**…where we contend with an even more ominous concentration

of demonic power: territorial spirits. Paul writes that "we do not wrestle against flesh and blood, but against principalities, against powers, against rulers of the darkness of this age, against hosts of wicked in heavenly places" (Eph. 6:12).[1]

Spiritual warfare was designed by Satan to put out the light of the believer. The enemy is strategic in his plan to annihilate everything in your life. Look at the following scripture:

"In whom the god of this world hath blinded the minds of them which believe not, lest the light of the glorious gospel of Christ, who is the image of God, should shine unto them."

Second Corinthians 4:4

As we follow God's plan, it is our obligation to remain free from the traps and manipulations of the enemy, because whom the Son sets free is free indeed. Once your house is swept clean, it must remain clean. It will only remain clean if we dwell in a place of fasting, prayer and humility.

In the next chapter, I will share testimonies of believers who were freed from the hand of the enemy's devices. Deliverance is available to anyone trapped in the relentless cycle of yielding to satanic traps.

> He teaches my hands to war, so that my arms can bend a bow of bronze.
> (Psalm 18:34)

When you come to a spiritual understanding of warfare, you will realize that the enemy is relentless in his pursuit of your destruction. You must be equally relentless in your pursuit of his downfall. You must not surrender any ground or territory to his evil devices. The only way to accomplish this is through the Word of God, a prayer life, a fasting lifestyle, and knowledge of Satan's art of warfare. All of which are covered by the full armor of God and the Blood of Jesus. Look at what it means to have a house swept clean.

The Art of Spiritual Warfare

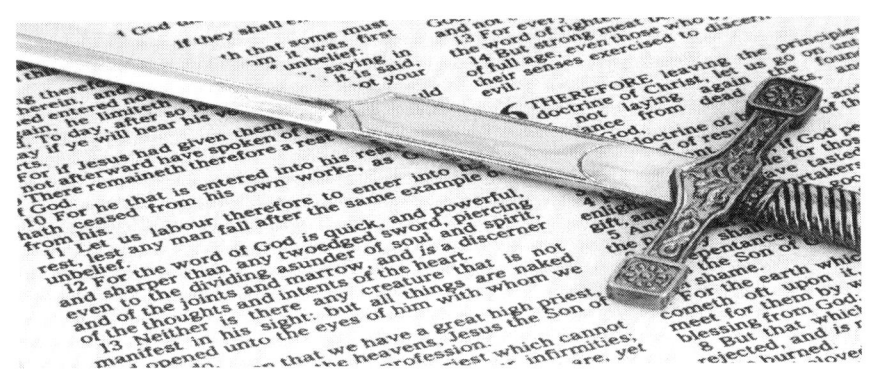

Chapter 4

A House Swept Clean

When God called me into ministry, the ministry of deliverance was one of the areas He chose. People often ask:

- ✓ Are demons real?
- ✓ How do I clean my house?
- ✓ What should I do when I see strange shadows and movements in my house?

- ✓ What are objects that leave doors open for satanic attacks?
- ✓ Can demons come into my house?
- ✓ How and what do I use to anoint my house?
- ✓ How do I close doors that allow the enemy access?

The list of questions and situations are more than we have time for in this book, but I pray that you get the idea. Here are several stories of individuals I have helped through the ministry of deliverance.

Tom and Grace: (Not their real names)
Tom and Grace were married and moved into a new house where they brought their property together. Grace began to feel uncomfortable in the new house, but she did not understand the reason for the discomfort. While Tom was away on business, the Lord instructed her to clean the storage room where Tom stored some boxes. Grace went through every item until she found the last

box tucked away in the back of the storage room. Inside the box was a brown paper bag and inside the brown paper bag was a plastic bag, which contained a "witchcraft spell" that was devised to draw Tom into a web of lust, manipulation and deceit. The "spell" was known as a potion or enchantment, which employs the forces of evil to achieve demonic results in the natural world, and Tom, was the target. She discovered it and immediately called for assistance.

I instructed her to take the package outside and place it in a grill or trash container in order to burn it completely. After it was burned, remove all the debris, place it back in the original container, and remove it from the premises. Anoint every place the satanic object touched and pray the Breaking Witchcraft Prayer. When Tom returned home, they prayed the Breaking Witchcraft Prayer and had no further problems.

Anointing oil is a substance made from olive oil and fragrant spices such as Frankincense and Myrrh. It is a symbol of healing, consecration and impartation. The oil is also a sign of God's invisible presence working on our behalf.

#2 Craig and his knife collection:

Craig is a collector of knives. Over the years, he collected beautiful antique knives and kept them in a glass case. After he surrendered his life to the Lord, he began to notice a series of unexplainable activities in the house. He called and asked for advice because he was seeing dark shadows in the house. After prayer, the Lord revealed that there were portals open in his house. We began the journey of "house cleaning." We fasted, prayed and anointed the house. Craig discovered that in every area of the house, there was peace, except in his bedroom, there he saw glimpses of shadows and figures. He called and again we prayed. The Lord revealed that the open portal was in the bedroom and it had to be closed if peace would come to the entire house. The enemy had a right to be there because his property was there.

Finally, the Lord showed us a knife in the case that was the portal for the demonic forces. After removing the knife and cleaning the house again, Craig finally had the peace of God resting in his physical and spiritual house. The "demonic object" contaminated Craig's knife collection and the remaining knives had to be anointed to complete the spiritual cleansing. "Demonically contaminated" objects can leave an open portal for satanic attacks. We must be careful when we bring objects into our homes or wear them on our body. Objects we deem harmless such as Craig's knife collection could in fact be a gateway for demonic activity.

#3 Karla (Not her real name) was being tormented every night. One evening I was with her for a ministry session and she fell asleep. We were on opposite sofas and I could see her as she relentlessly tossed and turned. I prayed and asked the Lord to show me what she was experiencing so that I could pray effectively.

Around 3:00 a.m. I started to dose off when suddenly; a small demonic figure began circling Karla tormenting her as she slept. As the demonic force continued, she became more disturbed. I asked the Lord to reveal the demon at work. The Lord replied, "A tormenting spirit." As I prayed, the spirit of torment flew out the window.

I started to fall asleep again when a tall grey figure, three figures in one appeared. I commanded them to identify themselves and they replied, "We are bitterness, unforgiveness and anger, and we have a right to be here."

Binding and casting out the enemy should be your first response when faced with demonic forces. The power of God's word says we have the authority given to us by Christ Jesus to heal the sick, raise the dead and *cast out demons.* Are you taking the authority you have been given? "And I will give unto thee the keys of the kingdom of heaven: and whatsoever thou shalt bind on earth shall be bound in heaven: and whatsoever thou shalt loose on earth shall be loosed in heaven" (Matthew 16:19). Are you binding and loosing?

The enemy is very legalistic and he knows his rights. They have a legal right to come against you when you are walking, living or breathing in their territory. He knows when you are operating in his territory and partaking of his evil fruit.

Finally, around 5 a.m. a final demon manifested. A tall dingy white figure appeared standing over Karla as if she was his property. I asked with a commanding voice, "Who are you?" The demon replied, "I am jealousy, the strongman." That did it! I grabbed my sword and anointing oil and began to war in the spirit on behalf of Karla. Accessing the authority given to me by Jesus, I prayed to our Heavenly Father, in the Name and authority of Jesus Christ and by the power of His shed Blood. Throughout the warfare, she never awoke. I prayed and anointed her with oil - head to toe. I anointed the room and began to cut demonic chains that had entrapped her. When Karla awoke, I was sitting upright, sword at my side, watching over her and greeting her with a smile. The Bible says that we must bear one another's burdens in Galatians 6:2: "Bear one another's burdens, and thereby fulfill the law of Christ."

For three nights, I bore Karla's burden in order to be the strength she needed to stand against the demonic forces warring against her. She had no idea that spiritual warfare was a reality and she was right in the middle of a battle for her life.

We cleaned the entire house and Karla entered a three day fast in order for God to deliver her from the strongholds, traps and snares of the enemy. Karla's life had been "contaminated" by the things she allowed into her eye and ear gates. She later told me that she never wanted to go back to her former state. She now knew that her entire lifestyle would have to change if the doors to the demonic activity were to remain closed.

#4 Amanda (Not her real name)

Amanda is an example of a life that does not hold on to the teachings and deliverance given by the Lord Jesus Christ. Matthew 12:43-45 states, *"Now when the unclean spirit goes out of a man, it passes through waterless places seeking rest, and does not find it. "Then it says, 'I will return to my house from which I came'; and when it comes, it finds it unoccupied, swept, and put in order. "Then it goes and takes along with it seven other spirits more wicked than itself, and they go in and live there; and the last state of that man becomes worse than the first. That is the way it will also be with this evil generation."*

During afternoon prayer, the Lord began to purge demonic spirits from Amanda. She coughed and purged (vomited) for what seemed like an hour.

☞

> Vomiting is an act of purging that takes place when a person is being a delivered. It is not the only indication of a person's deliverance. Other manifestations include but are not limited to shaking, belching, coughing, spitting, and foaming at the mouth, drooling, roaring or screaming.

A House Swept Clean

The Lord instructed me to call out the demons that held her captive. With the exposure of each demon, she continued to purge. It was not until the "spirit of pride" was called out that she withdrew and lay dormant on the floor. When she arose, she began to justify her reasons for purging. What happened? Pride shut down her deliverance (pride was her strongman). As we traveled home, I continued praying. She told me that she was feeling sick and asked if we could pull over. We found a service station and she went directly to the restroom. I stood outside the restroom praying, as she began purging again. I prayed calling out the demonic influences operating in her. Finally, she emerged from the restroom looking as if she had lost thirty pounds of spiritual weight.

> You have also given me the shield of Your salvation, And Your right hand upholds me; And Your gentleness makes me great.
> (Psalm 18:35)

We continued our journey and I counseled her on the

events that took place at prayer and in the restroom. I told her that God was cleaning her house and she must keep it clean and filled with the Word of God. I advised her to meet with her pastor and continue moving forward in her deliverance. The house was swept clean from the oppression of the enemy and now was the time to draw closer to the Lord through prayer, fasting and the Word of God.

Unfortunately, she did not listen to counsel and doorways that God closed were re-opened. Because pride was not addressed, doorways were re-opened and the "spirit of rebellion" raised his ugly head. She rejected counsel from her pastor and began a campaign of division and sabotage within her church.

Her latter condition was worse than her initial state because darkness covered her eyes, ears and mind. When you find your life being changed by the hand of

God, do not harden your heart as He begins to reveal the areas that are open doors for Satanic oppression. Jesus died so that we would have the right to abundant life and be free from the chains of bondage.

I believe that Amanda wanted to be free of the traps and manipulations of the enemy, but her ability fight was not strong enough to stand in the midst of the enemy's attack. She withdrew from the voice of the Lord, which meant she advanced towards the voice of the enemy. I say this because she insisted that she was fine and needed no additional counseling. It is tragic when a life with so much potential is infiltrated by the enemy and a systematic self-destructive assault begins. The spirits of pride and rebellion are like that. It is a challenging matter when the hidden strongholds are being exposed in your life. It is not easy to go through and you will either walk it out or reject it.

The enemy is out to kill, steal and destroy every area of your life. As the Lord begins to move in and through your life - walk it out, stay the course and do not look back. Arm yourself with the Word of God. Stand fast in prayer and fasting. Jesus said in Matthew 17:21, "But this kind does not go out except by prayer and fasting." John 8:36 declares that, "So if the Son makes you free, you will be free indeed." It is only when we are willing to face the truth and walk in it, we will be truly free. "And you will know the truth, and the truth will make you free" (John 8:32). FREEDOM has a price. Are you willing to pay?

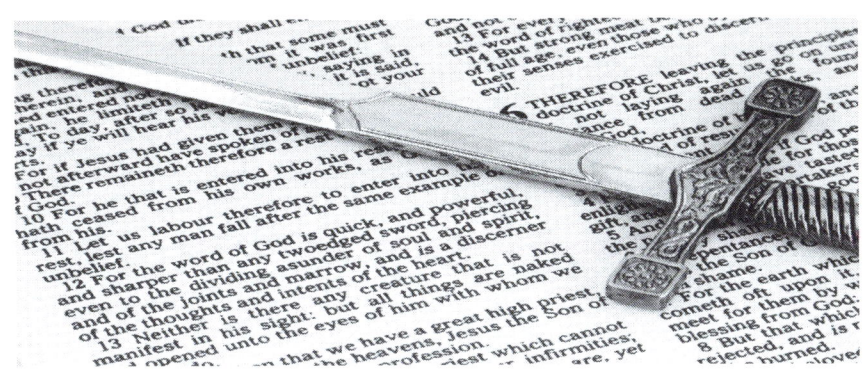

Chapter 5
Are You Armed and Ready?

As believers, we must be armed and ready for war. The enemy has a list of strategies and tactics to wage war against us. If we are going to defeat the enemy, we must know the manner in which his demonic forces operate.

Satan and his demonic forces are out to bind, blind, oppress, and deceive humanity. He is relentless in his attacks against us and he will not stop in his attempts to destroy our witness, purpose and destiny in Christ Jesus.

Ignorance is the enemy's first line of assault. He wields ignorance as a writer wields a pen. People are destroyed for lack of knowledge. The enemy will blind the eyes and hearts of man in order to keep us in bondage and spiritual darkness. Satan's dirty tactics are designed to keep humanity blind while he sabotages God's plan for us.

In order to bind and destroy the works of the enemy, you must first be able to recognize him. You must not be ignorant of Satan's devices and never give place or territory to him.

There is a movie entitled, "Invasion of the Body Snatchers" starring Donald Sutherland. In the movie, aliens infiltrated earth and began replacing humans with aliens birthed by way of a pod. The extraterrestrials assumed identical human appearance and began a plot to replace all human life with their alien counterparts. Just as the aliens sent their agents to sabotage and destroy human life, Satan sends his own dark forces to disrupt and destroy the church and its people. The demonic agents take on our appearance and speak our language, but their loyalty is to another kingdom, the kingdom of darkness. Just as a hand full of earthlings needed to detect the presence of aliens, the body of Christ needs to discern individuals operating under demonic influences.

Satan has many traps, deceptions, manipulations and snares in which to place humanity in bondage. The things that trapped you last year may not work this year. Satan has an arsenal of weapons and soldiers to dispatch against you. As you grow spiritually, the lowest rank of principalities will no longer be effective; Satan will then dispatch higher-ranking powers or captains. As you continue to grow spiritually, the demonic forces are moved up the hierarchical ladder as they are dispatched against you. As in any war, never send a private to do the job of a captain. It will not matter what he sends after you, when you are armed with the weapons of your warfare, you are a formidable warrior in the Lord's Army.

In chapter 9, we will discuss the works of the enemy and the weapons he will use in his attacks against you. Again, you must know your enemy if you are going to defeat him. The enemy wants to make war with you; therefore, you need to be prepared for the war. You will face certain defeat if you go into the battle unprepared. This is where this book comes in, to prepare you for the warfare that is being waged against you. Unfortunately, some of God's people fail to recognize there is a war being waged against them and they walk into the battle unprepared. That is why I believe Satan does not see some religions as a threat, because they don't take warfare seriously. We can see in Ephesians 6:11 that we must: *"Put on the whole armour of God that ye may be able to stand against the wiles of the devil."* Without the full armor of God, you are already defeated. Every believer is called to war and war is not a "you" or "me" thing – it is a "kingdom" thing, with kingdom principles that must be adhered to if we are to be more than conquerors. When a soldier goes into battle, he does not leave his arm or leg behind. His entire body must be properly trained to withstand the attacks of the enemy. Just as he must train and equip his physical body, he must also train and equip his emotional, mental and spiritual body to endure in the midst of the war.

As believers, we must train and equip *The Body* to

stand in the midst of the war. We must be properly equipped with the full armor of God, full knowledge of our enemy and full knowledge of ourselves. It is not enough to know your enemy you must also know yourself.

The worst thing a soldier can do is march into a battle believing he is armed and ready when in fact he is not. Why would you send a private to fight a general's battle? The line of attack of a general is more calculated and strategic than that of a private. In other words, a prayer private may not be equipped to war against spirits such as Jezebel. Why? Because a prayer private is still trying to establish a solid prayer life.

Being armed and ready for battle is not easy; it takes years of fasting, prayer, and studying the Word of God. Never send a novice into battle with a surface knowledge of the enemy.

To be **ARMED** means:
1. Equipped with one or more weapons.
2. Prepared and ready for use as a weapon.
3. Equipped with the information or tools needed to achieve something.[2]

ARE YOU ARMED with the Word of God, and with the knowledge of your enemy? Are you armed with the prayer life needed to stand and withstand? Are you prepared and ready to use the weapons of your warfare?

READY means:
1. Prepared for something that is going to happen.
2. Finished and available for use.
3. Quickly, easily given, provided, or available.
4. Prepared or blended in advance, and able to be used with very little additional preparation.
5. Intelligent, alert, and quick-witted.[3]

Are you **READY**? Are you ready for the attacks that are going to happen simply because you are a believer in Christ Jesus? Are you available to be used by our Commander In Chief? Are you prepared to stand and command?

It does not matter what your answer is, the fact that you are reading this book is a sure indication that you have a desire to become armed and ready to stand and take authority in the midst of the battle. I commend you for recognizing the need to be properly trained and for your desire to learn as much as possible about spiritual warfare.

In the midst of the war, age is not a factor, neither is our racial, social, economic or ethnic background. The enemy is no respecter of persons, he is out to kill, steal and destroy us and he has the demonic artillery needed to accomplish his goal. It is because of "whose we are" that he is out to destroy us. It is because we were bought with the price of the shed blood of Jesus. Therefore, we must take up the bloodstained banner and hold it up in victory because He has trained our hands for war and our fingers for battle.

In the next chapter, I want to introduce you to a 2000 year-old general who taught ordinary women how to become extraordinary soldiers, master strategist, General Sun Tzu.

The Art of Spiritual Warfare

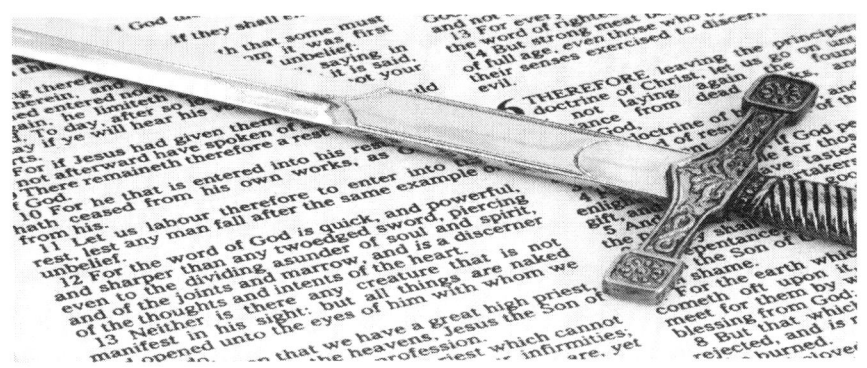

Chapter 6
Meet the General...

I enjoy the teachings of Sun Tzu in his book, *The Art of War*. His book appeals to individuals in the business world because it teaches strategies that can be applied to the boardroom. To many in the business world, the business of business often feels like warfare.

The Art of War teaches that the greatest victory is one

that does not require fighting a war. Translated, having done all to stand. What can the modern day reader\leader\believer learn from *The Art of War*, a manual that is over two thousand years old? A lot.

Sun Tzu was born around 544 BCE in the Qi State or Shondong Province. He was a third generation warrior; his father was a general and his grandfather a provincial governor. He was a brilliant military strategist, leading armies to great victories.

Sun Tzu's teachings have been instrumental in their ability to influence the war strategies of major countries such as Japan and it's unification; Napoleon and his European conquests; and American generals such as Douglas McArthur.

His teachings are affecting the way in which I view spiritual warfare. An effective warrior for the Kingdom must be armed and ready for the battle. We are told in Matthew 11:12, "And from the days of John the Baptist until now the kingdom of heaven suffereth violence and the violent take it by force." The Amplified Version translates it this way, "The kingdom of heaven has endured violent assault, and violent men seize it by force [as a precious prize—a share in the heavenly kingdom is sought with most ardent zeal and intense exertion]."

The bible is speaking of a "spiritual striving" for the Kingdom. Striving means to:

1. Trying hard to achieve or get something.
2. Fighting in opposition to something.
3. Competing resolutely against somebody or something.
4. Driven, motivated, and stirred.

My interest in the teachings of Sun Tzu came while

watching a television documentary on his life and teachings. Each time the commentator quoted General Sun's teachings, my spiritual ear responded with a spiritual counterpart. I became fascinated with his wisdom and began a quest to discover more about this brilliant military stragegist. His teachings carried a spiritual under tone that resonated in my belly.

I knew that the season would arrive when God would commission me to write another book on spiritual warfare. I also knew that as I grew spiritually, the teachings of Sun Tzu would become more relevant in my warfare strategies. When you can take the information you receive, make practical application to your life it becomes an area of growth and strength.

Even in the strangest or most difficult situations, always strive to learn from it. In every encounter always, strive to learn from your experiences, especially your mistakes. If you do not learn from your mistakes, you might repeat them.

There is an incident described in *The Art of War* that stands out as a real life lesson. The Duke of Wu commissioned Sun Tzu to turn his concubine (official mistress in some cultures) into warriors. When Sun Tzu gave a command to the women they smiled and giggled, but failed to respond to the command. Sun Tzu reasoned that either the commander did not make his commands clear or the ones receiving the commands were not clear on the orders given. He gave the command again and received the same results. Sun Tzu ordered the disobedient main concubines beheaded. After seeing the fate of anyone not following his commands, the remaining women fell in line and became powerful warriors.

The story has stayed with me to this day. Why? Because war is serious business, anyone trying to smile and giggle at Satan and his demonic forces will end up beheaded and left spiritually dead.

The forces of darkness that wage war against us are out for our total destruction. They want death and destruction to anyone and everything. They are out to kill, steal and destroy without reservation or hesitation.

Like the Duke of Wu's concubine who thought Sun Tzu was joking, some modern day believers think Satan is a pointed eared, pitchfork-carrying joke.

- ◆ God issues a command to fight - they smile and giggle.
- ◆ God says tithe - they spend or hoard their money.
- ◆ God calls for fasting and prayer - they eat and watch television.

◆ God says repent - they turn a deaf ear and continue in their sin.
◆ God says feed the poor - they heap to themselves.

The result, a state of rebellion and disobedience that opens doors for Satan to launch a full frontal attack. An attack arises that the rebellious believer is neither ready nor equipped for. It also gives the enemy access to behead your finances, your marriage, your children, your business or ministry. Failure to obey the voice of the Lord is dangerous and can be fatal.

> For our struggle is not against flesh and blood, but against the rulers, against the powers, against the world forces of this darkness, against the spiritual forces of wickedness in the heavenly places.
> (Ephesians 6:12)

Just as Sun Tzu got the women's attention by beheading the disobedient ones, God will allow things to happen in your life in order to get your attention. Remember, there are consequences to sin and disobedience. After you have been cut off from the blessings of God long enough, you will either line up with God and his commands or you will die in the wilderness of life.

Disobedience and rebellion must be addressed if we are to be successful warriors for the Kingdom, as well as be effective in our personal lives. Disobedient and rebellious soldiers will render the entire troop weak. We are only as strong as our weakest link. A church or ministry filled with rebellious individuals will prove to be a breeding ground for the advancement of Satan's kingdom. Scripture reveals that rebellion is as the sin of witchcraft: "For rebellion is as the sin of witchcraft, and stubbornness is as iniquity and idolatry" (First Samuel 15:23). Image having a church or ministry filled with rebellious individuals running around tearing down the work of the ministry and destroying the lives of unsuspecting sheep.

The Duke of Wu's women did not understand who was standing before them and as a result, several lost their lives. You must understand who is waging war against you; otherwise, you will be cut down.

Just as Sun Tzu was a formidable military warrior, Satan is also a formidable adversary in the war against you. You cannot take it for granted that he is misinformed when it comes to strategies and tactics that are designed to render you ineffective. Satan has real power and it would be wise to take him serious. He has studied humanity and he is armed with the knowledge and an endless arsenal of weapons. In addition, you must realize that you are not at war with flesh and blood; you are at war with an adversary that is in an entirely different realm, a demonic spiritual realm. In a later chapter, we will discuss buttons that he likes to push. It is time to unmask your greatest enemy and discover what you are fighting.

The Art of Spiritual Warfare

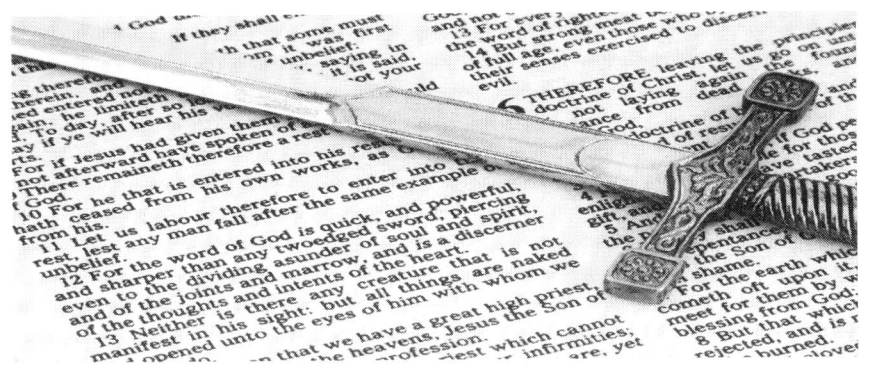

Chapter 7

What Are You Fighting?

You must understand spiritual warfare in order to be properly armed with the knowledge of your greatest enemy. It is not the person sitting next to you, it will not be the stranger on the streets and it is not your neighbor next door. Although the enemy may use them to come against you, you are not fighting the person; you are fighting the spirit operating through the person. The

Apostle Paul gives us a clear picture of what we are fighting against in his letter to the Ephesians: "For we wrestle not against flesh and blood, but against principalities, against powers, against the rulers of the darkness of this world, against spiritual wickedness in high places" (Ephesians 6:12). You are fighting against principalities, against powers, against rulers of the darkness and against spiritual wickedness in high places. The Apostle Paul warned the believers in Ephesus that they were in a spiritual battle against invisible armed forces of darkness. They were struggling against evil powers that were scheming to annihilate them.

I have studied Ephesians chapter 6 for years and one day the revelation of my true enemy hit me after facing a tough battle and feeling as if I was about to succumb to the constant bombardment of his attacks. It was through this verse that the eyes of my understanding opened and the birthing of this book began.

For we wrestle not against flesh and blood, but against principalities, against powers...

> Lest Satan should get an advantage of us: for we are not ignorant of his devices.
> (2 Corinthians 2:11)

The Greek translation of the word *principality* is derived from the word *ruler*. The word *power* is the word for *authority*. Simply stated, we are not fighting against a flesh and blood enemy, or contending with physical opponents, but against *rulers or rulerships* and the *kingdom or territory* of their *authority*.

against the rulers of the darkness of this world...

A better understanding of this verse would be, "Against the world rulers or leaders of this present darkness."

against spiritual wickedness in high places.

A better translation of this verse would read, "against the spirit forces of wickedness in the heavenly or supernatural realm." The Greek translation of "high places" is "heavenly."

I believe that in some cases we also have a misunderstanding about the place where Satan is seated. Just as some of us picture Satan sporting a pitchfork, wagging a long pointed tail and having horns protruding from his head, we also envision him in hell at the center of the earth. None of which is true. Ephesians 2:2 states that Satan is the "prince of the power of the air." "Wherein in time past ye walked according to the course of this world, according to the ***prince of the power of the air***, the spirit that now worketh in the children of disobedience" (Ephesians 2:2). Satan is NOT in the belly of the earth neither is he in the heaven of heavens, the third heaven residing with God, the Father. Satan resides in the "heavenly" realm, the second heaven.

"For we wrestle not against flesh and blood, but against principalities, against powers, against the rulers of the darkness of this world, against spiritual wickedness in high places" (Ephesians 6:12).

We are not fighting against a flesh and blood enemy, or contending with physical opponents, but against rulers or leaders and the kingdom or territory of their authority, against the world rulers or rulership of this present darkness, against the spiritual forces of wickedness in the heavenly realm. Take a closer look at the spiritual insurgents that are waging war against us. It is always helpful to know as much about your enemy as possible.

The spirit forces of wickedness that we are fighting are defined in The Dake Annotated Reference Bible as:

1. Gr. <u>archas</u>, principalities, chief rulers or beings of the highest rank and order in Satan's kingdom. (v.12; 1:21; Col. 2:10)

2. Gr. <u>exousias</u>, authorities, those who derive their power from and execute the will of the chief rulers. (v. 12; 1:21; Col. 2:10)

3. Gr. <u>kosmokratopas</u>, world rulers of the darkness of this age, the spirit world-rulers. (v. 12; 1:21; Col. 2:10)

4. Gr. <u>pneumatika ponerias</u>, spiritual wickedness, that of the wicked spirits of Satan in the heavenly realm. (v. 12; 1:21; Col. 1:16-18)

As you rightly divide the word of God, you will receive a greater understanding and your warfare strategies will grow because you are renewing your mind to spiritual warfare, your archenemy and his spiritual rebels.

Ephesians chapter 6 will mean nothing if you have not proven your battle attire. David told Saul that he could not wear the armor of Saul because it was not tested.

> "Then Saul clothed David with his garments and put a bronze helmet on his head, and he clothed him with armor. David girded his sword over his armor and tried to walk, for he had not tested them. David said to Saul, "I cannot go with these, for I have not tested them." And David took them off" (1 Samuel 17:38-39 NASB).

Battle attire will not be effective until you have tested, studied and applied it to your life. You can sit and hear the word of God week after week and never apply it to your life and you will end up living a defeated life. The Lord spoke these words one evening during prayer, *"many people have never tasted victory because they have never tasted Me."* Victory comes when we have tasted the Lord in our lives. Oh, taste and see…

Ephesians chapter 6 will be a part of your battle cry when you rightly divide it for yourself. We must come to a spiritual understanding of the battlefield because our lives depend on it. It is time to be transformed by renewing your mind and move to another level or dimension of spiritual warfare.

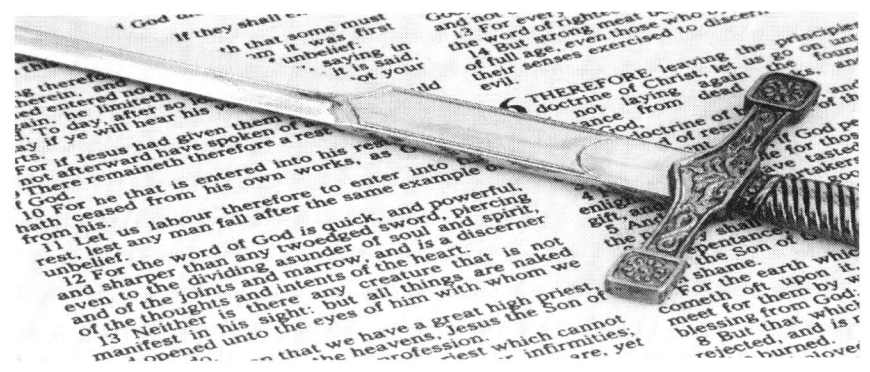

Chapter 8
The Battlefield is YOUR MIND!

Every battle must have a battlefield, the place where opposing forces meet to engage the conflict. In spiritual warfare, the battlefield is your mind. Your mind is the center of consciousness that generates thoughts, feelings, ideas, and perceptions, and stores knowledge and memories.

Since the battle begins in the mind, the battlefield of the mind must be fortified. The mind is where the enemy sets up strongholds, a mental, spiritual or physical place of bondage. Strongholds in spiritual warfare are made up of deeply rooted thought patterns that are dominated by three opposing forces. They are:

1. Habits or desires or lusts
2. Worldly thinking
3. Demonic manipulations

Satan utilizes whatever is at his disposal to bring about our destruction. Since the battle begins in the mind, he will use our desires, physical needs or appetites, to destroy us. "For all that is in the world, the lust of the flesh, and the lust of the eyes, and the pride of life, is not of the Father, but is of the world" (1 John 2:16).

LUST OF THE FLESH

The *lust of the flesh* includes: sexual immorality, impurity and debauchery; idolatry and witchcraft; hatred, discord, jealousy, fits of rage, selfish ambition, dissensions, factions and envy; drunkenness, orgies, theft, murder, adultery, greed, malice, deceit, lewdness, envy, slander, arrogance and folly (Galatians 5:19-21, Mark 7:21-23).

In spiritual warfare, the battle begins in the mind and as you can see from Galatians and Mark, the works of the flesh all begin with a thought, curiosity or suggestion. The thought is planted in the mind before the actual deed is carried out.

LUST OF THE EYES

What is lust of the eyes? How does a person sin with the eyes? Scripture teaches that the eyes lust for many things.

Sex

But I say to you that everyone who looks at a woman with lust for her has already committed adultery with her in his heart (Matthew 5:28).

Evil

But if your eyes are bad, your whole body will be full of darkness. If then the light within you is darkness, how great is that darkness! (Matthew 6:23).

Material Things

Then He said to them, "Beware, and be on your guard against every form of greed; for not even when one has an abundance does his life consist of his possessions" (Luke 12:15).

Pleasures of this world

All that my eyes desired I did not refuse them. I did not withhold my heart from any pleasure, for my heart was pleased because of all my labor and this was my reward for all my labor (Ecclesiastes 2:10).

Other gods

'You shall not make for yourselves idols, nor shall you set up for yourselves an image or a sacred pillar, nor shall you place a figured stone in your land to bow down to it; for I am the LORD your God (Leviticus 26:1). Society would have us to believe that we need all these things to be happy and fulfilled. It is not the desire that is wrong; it is when the desire, person, or object becomes an obsession or "your god."

THE PRIDE OF LIFE

Pride is defined as a haughty attitude shown by somebody who believes, often unjustifiably, that he or she is better than others are. The pride of life places its victim in a vacuum of self-centeredness. The pride of life is a device of the enemy that focuses the mind and thoughts primarily on the person and his needs. A person walking in the pride of life:

- Seeks attention through dress or looks
- Seeks attention through rank or wealth
- Seeks honor
- Seek recognition
- Seeks fame
- Seeks power
- Seek position
- Seeks luxury
- Seeks wealth for recognition and power
- Seeks to outshine others
- Seeks importance [4]

As you can see, the enemy will use US against US! The warfare begins in the mind and the enemy knows how to strategically place before us a buffet table filled with enticements, inducements, seductions, attractions or **BAIT**, to ignite a deadly firestorm in our flesh for the things of this world through the lust of the flesh, lust of the eyes and the pride of life. He cannot make you BITE THE BAIT, but he can entice you through your need for self-indulgence, self-sufficiency, self-glory, self-righteousness, or self-importance.

Once the fire is ignited, it will take the power of God to deliver you from the enemy within you. The lust of the flesh, lust of the eyes and the pride of life are designed to stop the flow of God in your life. "For all that is in the world, *the lust of the flesh and the lust of the eyes and the boastful pride of life*, is not from the Father, but is from the world. The world is passing away, and also its lusts; but the one who does the will of God lives forever." (1John 2:16-17 italics added).

Our prayer should be, "Lord deliver me, from me." "We must pray daily, Search me, O God, and know my heart; test me and know my anxious thoughts. See if there is any offensive way in me, and lead me in the way everlasting" (Psalm 139:23-24 NIV).

Let's turn our attentions to the devices, strategies and doctrines of Satan that can lure us into his web of lies, deceits, seductions and death.

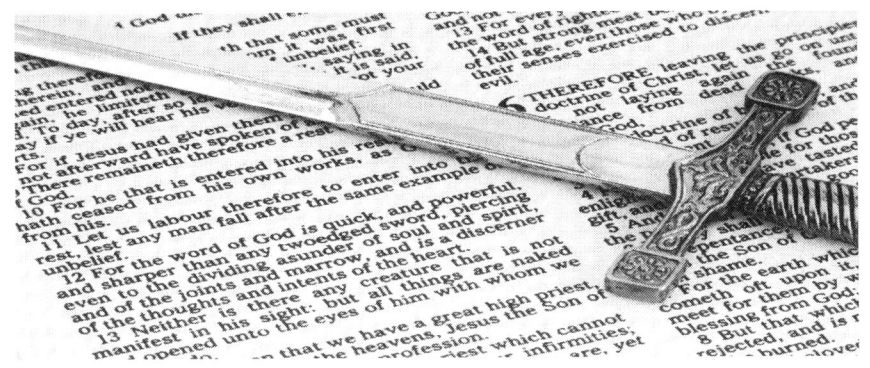

Chapter 9
The Devices & Doctrines of Satan

Every well-armed soldier should know his weaponry, know the territory and know his enemy. Without accurate knowledge of the enemy, you are headed for defeat. The media portrays Satan and his demonic forces as mystical, entertaining, deceptive, powerful, seductive, sensuous and brilliant. While at the same time portraying Jesus Christ as weak, uninformed, laughable, gullible and powerless.

There are components vital to your arsenal for effective spiritual warfare that will tear down these misconceptions. They will guide you in your battle against the deceptive tricks and manipulations of the enemy. Satan is the minister of propaganda and he uses his propaganda machine to deceive humanity into believing that he is in control of the destiny of humanity. He wields his propaganda machine - doubt, unbelief, fear, lies, and doctrinal error with demonic precision. I believe that our biggest act of ignorance is not studying and applying the Word of God. Ignorance comes from being uninformed, ill informed, unfamiliar, oblivious, unknowing, unenlightened, inexperienced, unaware or illiterate.

The Bible warns us against being ignorant of Satan's devices. Therefore, we must be knowledgeable when it comes to his strategies that are designed to kill, steal and destroy. First John 3:8 informs us, "The one who practices sin is of the devil; for the devil has sinned from the beginning. The Son of God appeared for this purpose, to destroy the works of the devil." When properly armed with the Word of God, we can dispel the lies and misconceptions about Satan and his demonic forces. It is time to arm ourselves.

Satan's Origin:

Satan was created by the Lord along with other beings, principalities and powers in the heavenly and earth realm (Job 38:4-7; Ezekiel 28:11-17; Col. 1:15-18).

"Where were you when I laid the foundation of the earth? Tell Me, if you have understanding, Who set its measurements? Since you know. Or who stretched the line on it? "On what were its bases sunk? Or who laid its cornerstone, When the morning stars sang together and all the sons of God shouted for joy" (Job 38:4-7)?

"Again the word of the LORD came to me saying, "Son of man, take up a lamentation over the king of Tyre and say to him, 'Thus says the Lord GOD, "You had the seal of perfection, full of wisdom and perfect in beauty. "You were in Eden, the garden of God; Every precious stone was your covering: The ruby, the topaz and the diamond; The beryl, the onyx and the jasper; The lapis lazuli, the turquoise and the emerald; And the gold, the workmanship of your settings and sockets, was in you. On the day that you were created, They were prepared. "You were the anointed cherub who covers, and I placed you there. You were on the holy mountain of God; You walked in the midst of the stones of fire. "You were blameless in your ways from the day you were created until unrighteousness was found in you. "By the abundance of your trade, you were internally filled with violence, and you sinned; Therefore, I have cast you as profane from the mountain of God. And I have destroyed you, O covering cherub, From the midst of the stones of fire. "Your heart was lifted up because of your beauty; You corrupted your wisdom by reason of your splendor. I cast you to the ground; I put you before kings, That they may see you" (Ezekiel. 28:11-17).

"He is the image of the invisible God, the firstborn of all creation. For by Him all things were created, both in the heavens and on earth, visible and invisible, whether thrones or dominions or rulers or authorities — all things have been created through Him and for Him. He is before all things, and in Him, all things hold together. He is also head of the body, the church; and He is the beginning, the firstborn from the dead, so that He Himself will come to have first place in everything" (Colossians 1:15-18).

Destroying Misconceptions About Satan

We must destroy misconceptions about Satan:

Satan is not:
1. An intangible power.
2. Sporting hoofs, horns, a tail, a pitchfork.
3. Presiding over a lake of fire.
4. A fabrication in man's mind.
5. Wandering beneath the earth's core.
6. Interested in negotiating with humanity.
7. A fan of man.
8. To be celebrated and honored.

What Satan is

E.M. Bounds affirms: "To Christ the devil was a very real person. He recognized his personality, felt and acknowledged his power, abhorred his character, and warred against his kingdom."[5] We must also be aware of his personality, power, character and kingdom.

1. Satan is a real person.
   - 1 Chronicles 21:1; Job 1:6-12; Psalm 109:6; Zechariah 3:1-2; 1 Peter 5:8-9; Revelation 12:9-12

2. Satan has a kingdom.
   - Mark 3:22-26
3. Jesus dealt with him as with a person.
   - Matthew 4:1-11; Luke 4:1-13
4. Personal description given of him.
   - Isaiah 14:12-14; Ezekiel. 28:11-17
5. Jesus waged war on Satan.
   - Luke 13:16; Acts 10:38; 1 John 3:8
6. Apostles fought with Satan.
   - 1 Thessalonians 2:18; 1 Peter 5:8-9
7. He was described as a beautiful creature that fell because of pride.
   - Ezekiel 28:11-17; 1 Timothy 3:6
8. Satan is a celestial (heavenly) and terrestrial (earthly) ruler.
   - John 12:31; 2 Cor. 4:4; Ephesians 2:2
9. He has an organized kingdom of principalities, powers and rulers.
   - Matthew 12:25-30; Ephesians 6:10-12
10. He is the head of some religions.
    - 2 Corinthians 3:9

The Fall of Satan:
Satan fell because of pride over his own beauty and

trying to exalt himself above God. Ezekiel chapter 28 gives us a picture of the fall of Satan: "Again the word of the LORD came to me saying, "Son of man, take up a lamentation over the king of Tyre and say to him, 'Thus says the Lord GOD, "You had the seal of perfection, Full of wisdom and perfect in beauty. "You were in Eden, the garden of God; Every precious stone was your covering: The ruby, the topaz and the diamond; The beryl, the onyx and the jasper; The lapis lazuli, the turquoise and the emerald; And the gold, the workmanship of your settings and sockets, Was in you. On the day that you were created, They were prepared. "You were the anointed cherub who covers, And I placed you there. You were on the holy mountain of God; You walked in the midst of the stones of fire.

"You were blameless in your ways From the day you were created Until unrighteousness was found in you. "By the abundance of your trade, You were internally filled with violence, And you sinned; Therefore, I have cast you as profane From the mountain of God. And I have destroyed you, O covering cherub, From the midst of the stones of fire. "Your heart was lifted up because of your beauty; You corrupted your wisdom by reason of your splendor. I cast you to the ground; I put you before kings, That they may see you" (Ezekiel 28:11-17). Also First Timothy 3:6 warns us of the dangers of pride and conceit, "And not a new convert, so that he will not become conceited and fall into the condemnation incurred by the devil." Finally, Isaiah 14:12-14 gives us the clearest picture of all of the fall of Satan: "How you have fallen from heaven, O star of the morning, son of the dawn! You have been cut down to the earth, You who have weakened the nations! "But you said in your heart, 'I will ascend to heaven; I will raise my throne above the stars of God, And I will sit on the mount of assembly in the recesses of the north. 'I will ascend above the heights of the clouds; I will make myself like the Most High.'"

Pride was his weakness and his downfall. Pride can also be our weakness and downfall if we do not remain in a broken and contrite (repentant) place in God. "The sacrifices of God are a broken spirit; A broken and a contrite heart, O God, You will not despise" (Psalm 51:17). "For thus says the high and exalted One Who lives forever, whose name is Holy, "I dwell on a high and holy place, And also with the contrite and lowly of spirit in order to revive the spirit of the lowly and to revive the heart of the contrite" (Isaiah 57:15).

Satan's Names and Titles:

Throughout the Bible many names and titles are given to Satan such as the ones listed below:

Names of Satan	Scripture Reference
Abaddon	Revelation 9:11

The Devices & Doctrines of Satan

Accuser of the brethren	Revelation 12:10
Adversary	1 Peter 5:8-9
Angel of the bottomless pit	Revelation 9:11
Angel of light	2 Cor. 11:14
Beelzebub	Matthew 12:24
Belial	2 Corinthians 6:15
Devil	1 Peter 5:8
Dragon	Revelation 20:2
Enemy	Matthew 13:39
Father of lies	John 8:44
God of this world	2 Corinthians 4:4
Great dragon	Revelation 12:9
Lucifer	Isaiah 14:12-14
Murderer	John 8:44
Prince of devils	Matthew 12:24
Prince of power of the air	Ephesians 2:2
Prince of this world	John 14:30
Ruler of darkness	Ephesians 6:12
Ruler of this world	John 12:31
Serpent	Revelation 12:9
Tempter	1 Thess. 3:5

Wicked One   Matthew 13:19

The Work of Satan:

The enemy has a work to accomplish on the earth, but his primary goal is to oppose God whenever he can. From the Old Testament until this present age, Satan has had a wide range of objectives in relation to the opposition to God's Kingdom agenda. Ranging from the fall of man through Adam to preventing Jesus from coming to earth to fulfill His destiny of destroying the works of Satan. Here are ten primary works of Satan and although his list is endless, I pray that this hit list will open the doors and eyes of your understanding to the work of the enemy that rages against you.

Satan's Work

1. **Provokes men to Sin.**
   "And Satan stood up against Israel, and provoked David to number Israel" (1Chr. 21:1).

2. **Uses hardships to bring unbelief, rebellion and cold hearts towards Jesus.**
"But the younger widows refuse: for when they have begun to wax wanton against Christ, they will marry; Having damnation, because they have cast off their first faith. And withal they learn to be idle, wandering about from house to house; and not only idle, but tattlers also and busybodies, speaking things, which they ought not. I will therefore that the younger women marry, bear children, guide the house, give none occasion to the adversary to speak reproachfully. For some are already turned aside after Satan" (1Timothy 5:11-15).

3. **Causes sickness and disease.**
"How God anointed Jesus of Nazareth with the Holy Ghost and with power: who went about doing good, and healing all that were oppressed of the devil; for God was with him" (Acts 10:38).

4. **Causes doubt and unbelief.**
"And he that doubteth is damned if he eat, because he eateth not of faith: for whatsoever is not of faith is sin" (Romans 14:23).

5. **The deceiver of all men.**
"And the great dragon was cast out, that old serpent, called the Devil, and Satan, which

deceiveth the whole world: he was cast out into the earth, and his angels were cast out with him (Rev 12:9).

6. Robs men of the Word of God.
"When any one heareth the word of the kingdom, and understandeth it not, then cometh the wicked one, and catcheth away that which was sown in his heart. This is he which received seed by the way side" (Matthew 13:19).

7. Blinds men to the gospel.
"In whom the god of this world hath blinded the minds of them which believe not, lest the light of the glorious gospel of Christ, who is the image of God, should shine unto them" (2 Corinthians 4:4).

8. Tempts men.
And he was there in the wilderness forty days, tempted of Satan; and was with the wild beasts; and the angels ministered unto him" (Mark 1:13).

9. He is the leader of sinners.
"He who does what is sinful is of the devil, because the devil has been sinning from the beginning. The reason the Son of God appeared was to destroy the devil's work. No one who is born of God will continue to sin, because God's seed remains in him; he cannot go on sinning,

because he has been born of God. This is how we know who the children of God are and who the children of the devil are: Anyone who does not do what is right is not a child of God; nor is anyone who does not love his brother" (1John 3:8-10).

10. Makes war on the people of God.
"Put on the whole armour of God that ye may be able to stand against the wiles of the devil. For we wrestle not against flesh and blood, but against principalities, against powers, against the rulers of the darkness of this world, against spiritual wickedness in high places" (Eph 6:11-12).

Characteristics of Satan:

As with any person, Satan has characteristics that we must address in order to get a more comprehensive picture of his make up. He hates God and all of humanity with an evil passion and therefore he is unprincipled in his mission to obliterate everything that God created. He is:

Accuser of Man	Revelation 12:10
Aggressive	1 Peter 5:8-9
Adversarial	1 Peter 5:8-9

As a roaring lion	1 Peter 5:8-9
Coward	James 4:7
Counterfeiter	2 Thessalonians 2:9
Corrupt	Ezekiel 28:17
Cruel	1 Peter 5:8-9
Cunning	2 Corinthians 2:11
Deceitful	2 Corinthians 11:14
Deluder	2 Thessalonians 2:8-12
Devourer	1 Peter 5:8-9
Destroyer	John 10:10
Fierce	Luke 8:29
Iniquitous	Ezekiel 28:15
Lawless	2 Thessalonians 2:8-12
Liar	John 8:44
Murderer	John 8:44
Prideful	Genesis 28:17
Profane	Ezekiel 28:16
Schemer	2 Corinthians 2:11
Sinner	Ezekiel 28:16

Slanderer	Genesis 3:1-10
Sower of discord	Matthew 13:39
Tempter	Matthew 4:1-11
Thief	John 10:10
Violent	Ezekiel 28:16
Wicked	Luke 8:12

Methodology of Satan:

Every soldier has a method to his warfare and Satan is no different. He is very methodical in his traps, schemes and manipulations because his has had half an eternity to study humanity and he is an expert with his demonic weapons of warfare.

E.M. Bounds wrote in his book, *Guide to Spiritual Warfare*:

> Satan has the wisdom of an archangel and the experience of half an eternity as the captain of all the hosts of hell. He is an expert in the acts and art

of deception and trickery. He has almost inexhaustible resources at his command to serve his purposes. Other than God Himself, a wiser and more powerful spirit than Satan does not live. A more malicious power than he could not exist. There is no greater worker than he. His endless energy and tireless perseverance are the only things in him worthy of imitation. These things make him so powerful and dreadful.

Satan, the captain of hell, has laid out a battle plan designed to destroy humanity and render us ineffective for the Kingdom of God. His methods include:

1. Traps and snares to keep men in bondage.
2. Lies to keep men from turning to God.
3. Assaults to kill the believer's testimony.
4. Seducing believers into a lukewarm state.
5. Making sin look enticing.
6. Sends spirit of suicide to destroy souls of men.

7. Makes serving the Lord look boring.
8. Trying to lead churches into compromise.
9. Trying to make material things more important than spiritual things.
10. Urging churches to add more entertaining, alluring and worldly music in order to attract and distract individuals.
11. Urging leaders to preach a watered down gospel to keep attendees entertained.
12. Enticing believers to seek worldly forms of ministry as a way of spiritual enlightenment.
13. Blinding leaders to spirits such as Jezebel or Ahab when they infiltrate the church.
14. Enticing unqualified individuals to seek positions, titles, and offices as a way of self-exaltation.
15. Enticing leaders to become life coaches\motivational speakers instead of pastors\teachers\evangelists.

16. Making ministry appear glamorous resulting in the spirit of competition infiltrating the church.
17. Enticing leaders to allow moneymaking schemes into the church under the disguise of fundraisers, charitable outreaches and empowerment programs.
18. Enticing believers to seek spiritual wisdom through self-help groups, philosophy, world religions, mysticism and astrology.
19. Bringing religious condemnation to ministers that preach the uncompromising Word of God. Causing them to be outcasts in the religious community.
20. Bringing the spirits of heaviness or discouragement to true leaders in order to render them ineffective.

Make no mistake, Satan has a work to do against humanity and he makes every effort to oppose God and destroy everything that possesses the Breath of God. It is his job to make war against us. "And it was given unto him to make war with the saints, and to overcome them: and power was given him over all kindreds, and tongues, and nations. And all that dwell upon the earth shall worship him, whose names are not written in the book of life of the Lamb slain from the foundation of the world" (Revelation 13:7-9). You must grasp a firm understanding of your enemy, his tactics and strategies in order to be an effective soldier in the army of the Lord. It is vital that you have a firm knowledge of the rank and file (the enlisted troops in a military organization, excluding officers) of the enemy.

Demons and Unclean Spirits

We must have a firm understanding of Satan's demons and unclean spirits. We must know their nature, works and methods of operation. Satan has an army of demons at his command, ready to attack believers. Look at the demonology of Satan's assault team.

Definition:

The word demon means devil or spirit regarded as evil. Satan is the prince of demons as stated in Matthew 9:34: "But the Pharisees said, It is by the prince of demons that he drives out demons." Demons are disembodied spirits and cannot work in the natural world except through the possession of men or animals.

Nature of Demons

By their very nature they are evil, intelligent, powerful, not angels and yet not human. Demons have knowledge, doctrines, powers, emotions and desires. Make no mistake, they are organized and possess a disciplined military with one very evil commander - Satan. They carry out his orders with precision and obedience.

The Work of Demons

Demons also have a work to accomplish in the lives of the human race. They possess people and accomplish their work through the following:

Work of Demons	Scripture Reference
Anger	Genesis 4:5-7
Blindness	Matthew 12:22
Betrayals	John 13:2; 1 Kings 22:21-22
Bondage	Romans 8:15
Convulsions	Mark 9:20
Deceptions	1 Timothy 4:1-2
Discord	Matthew 13:36-43
Error	1 John 4:1-6
False Prophecy	1 Samuel 18:8-10
False Worship	Leviticus 17:7
Fear	2 Timothy 1:7
Jealousy	1 Samuel 16:14
Love of the World	1John 2:15-17

Love of Money	1 Timothy 6:10
Lying	1 Kings 22:21-24
Mute	Matthew 12:22
Oppression	Acts 10:38
Persecution	1 Peter 5:8
Sickness\Disease	Matthew 4:23-24
Sin	John 8:44; 1 John 3:8
Strength	Mark 5:1-18
Torment	Matthew 4:23-24
Wickedness	Luke 11:26
Witchcraft	2 Chronicles 33:6
Vexation	Matthew 15:22
Worry	Matthew 6:27-34

Weapons of the Enemy

Abortion	Leviticus 20:1-5; Amos 1:3 Molech, Spirit of Ammon
Abuse	Offense, criticism, control
Addiction	Obsession, compulsion
Adultery	Lust, unfaithful, 2 Peter 2; 14
Adversity	Hardships, Proverbs 24:10; Col. 1:24
Anger	Hatred, rage, Genesis 49:6-7
Anxiety	Worry, Philippians 4:6
Argumentative	Quarrelsome, 2 Timothy 2:23
Arrogance	Conceited, ego, (Ps. 89:10)
Backbiting	Lying, gossip, 2 Cor. 12:20
Besetting Sin	Hebrews 12:1
Bitterness	Jeremiah 4:18; Heb 12:15
Bondages	Exodus 13:3
Cares of world	Matthew 13:22
Complacency	1 Cor. 15:34; Eph. 5:14
Competition	Ambition, pride, jealousy

Contaminated Anointing	Jude 10-13
Condemnation	Guilt, Romans 8:1
Control	Possessiveness, witchcraft
Deception	Joshua 9:1-12; 2 Tim 3:13
Delusion	2 Thess. 11
Depression	Psalm 69:20; Psalm 119:28 Matthew 26:38
Discouragement	Psalm 42:5
Divination	Witchcraft Ex. 22:18; Deu. 18:10, Jeremiah 27:9
Double-minded	James 1:6-8
Doubt	Gen 3:1-7; Mark 11:23
False Burdens	Matthew 11:29-30
False entitlement	1 Kings 21:1-16
Fear	Job 3:25; 2 Tim. 4:17 1 John 4:18
Frustration	Defeat, Ezra 4:1-5
Generational Curses	Ex. 20:5; Num. 14:18; Deu. 11:26-28
Gossip	James 3:5-6; 1 Tim 5:13
Greed	Lust, selfishness, Eph 4:19

Hatred	Dislike, 1 John 3:15
Homosexuality	Uncleanness, Romans 1:5-28
Idolatry	Psalm 97:7
Incest	Lust, perversion Genesis 19:30-37
Insecurity	Low self esteem, shyness Exodus 3:9-12
Jealousy\Envy	Proverbs 6:34; SOS 8:6
Judgmental	James 4:11-12
Laziness	Idleness Proverbs 26:13-14
Lies	1 Timothy 4:1-2
Lusts	Gal. 5:16; James 1:14-15 2 Peter 2:18; 1 John 2:16
Manipulation	Control, deceit, lying
Oppression	Heaviness Acts 10:38; Ex 22:29
Negativity	Numbers 14:26-34
Perversions	Proverbs 17:20; Gen. 19:1-11
Poverty	Ruth 1:21; Psalm 12:5
Pride	Proverbs 11:2; 16:28
Rape	Judges 19:22-28

Rebellion	1 Samuel 15:23
Rejection	Mark 8:31; 12:10
Resentment	Genesis 4:1-8
Sabotage	Nehemiah 6:1-6
Seduction	2 Kings 21:9; Ezekiel 13:10
Shame	2 Samuel 13:12; 14:20
Sin	1 John 3:4
Snares	1 Samuel 18:21-25
Strongholds	Romans 1:21; Ephesians 4:18 2 Corinthians 10:4
Stumbling blocks	Ezekiel 14:3-4; 1 Peter 2:8 1 John 2:10; Rev. 2:14
Suicidal Thoughts	Matthew 26:38; 1 Kings 19:1-4
Suicide	Matthew 17:15
Unbelief	Matthew 13:58; Heb 4:1-2, 11
Uncleanness	Mark 1:23, 26-27
Unforgiveness	Mark 11:25-26

With the eyes of our understanding open to the facts about demons and unclean spirits, it is imperative that as soldiers of the Lord, we discern, test, resist and reject them. We must not allow them to gain ground in our lives. We must exercise every weapon in our arsenal in order to fight against them. We must use prayer, fasting, worship and the whole armor of God in our spiritual warfare.

We must recognize when demonic forces are operating in individuals around us. We must also recognize and destroy unholy alliances that we have allowed to form. As soldiers, we must steadily advance for the Kingdom of God and this will only be accomplished when we are well armed with the proper weapons of war.

Now that You Know:

You are now armed with the weapons of the enemy's warfare against us: Satan's origin, what he is and is not, his fall, his names and titles, his demons and unclean spirits, and his work against humanity. It is time to move forward and learn warfare strategies that will help you wage war with confidence and obedience to your Commander In Chief, Jesus Christ. *If any man has an ear, let him hear.*

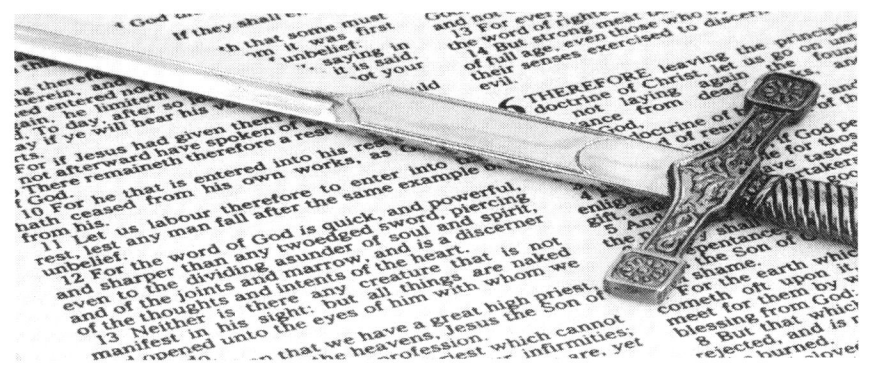

Chapter 10

Worldly Warfare vs. Spiritual Warfare

In our knowledge driven society, a society that says, "the more you have, the more successful you are," Sun Tzu's *The Art of War* stresses the importance of character and knowledge as the keys to success.

Sun Tzu's Perspective on War

Sun Tzu taught that wise leaders could not rely solely

on knowledge of the terrain or the capabilities of the opposition, but they had to know themselves. He taught that in order to be invincible, leaders had to develop a deep understanding of their own readiness, whether faced with praise or blame. General Sun Tzu taught that victory came to those who had developed an ethic of constant refinement and improvement. Finally, Sun Tzu said, "In war there is no fixity." In other words, when a leader devises a plan he must possess the ability to adapt. An effective leader is in tune to the timing and season of the war.

The Spiritual Perspective on the Art of War

In a spirit led society where spiritual weaknesses such as bondages, strongholds or sins are often hidden; the spiritual stance is exposed by the leader's ability or inability to engage spiritual warfare. In other words, if I am struggling with lust, I am not the vessel effective to fight against lust. If I am warring with bitterness, I am not a tool the Master can use to bring freedom to a bitter individual.

Wise leaders do not rely on worldly knowledge of the terrain or the capabilities of their enemy (Satan), but they get to know themselves through the eyes of God. "Search me, O God, and know my heart: try me, and know my thoughts: And see if there be any wicked way in me, and lead me in the way everlasting" (Psalm 139:23-24).

In order for a spirit led leader to be mighty through God, able to pull down strongholds, he needs to develop a deep understanding of his own readiness to fast, pray and seek the face of God. A spirit led leader is not concerned with the praises of man, his concern and ultimate goal is advancing the Kingdom of God and the glory of God.

Victory comes to those who are ready to stand in the midst of adversity. Standing with the full armor of God and having proven the armor, ready for the battle with complete confidence in their Commander in Chief.

In spiritual warfare, there are no "religious fixities." A spiritual warrior goes before the throne of grace seeking God for the direction of the battle. The spirit led leader flows with synchronized (coordinated) and syncopated (rhythmic) movements of the Spirit of the Living God.

A spirit led warrior is able to discern the times and seasons of the war. He stays in tune with the Lord through fasting and prayer. He knows when to advance, when to retreat, when to stand and when to fight. He understands the times and seasons as the Lord directs them, and stays in constant communication, trusting the Lord to bring victory.

The next chapter will focus on Sun Tzu's teachings from *The Art of War*. I will compare several of his teachings with the biblical perspective. If you keep an open mind, I believe you can learn a lot from his military strategies.

It is my prayer that you become a spiritual warfare strategist, able to face the enemy without fear or trepidation. No weapon formed against us will prosper as long as we are armed with the proper weapons for the warfare.

The Art of Spiritual Warfare

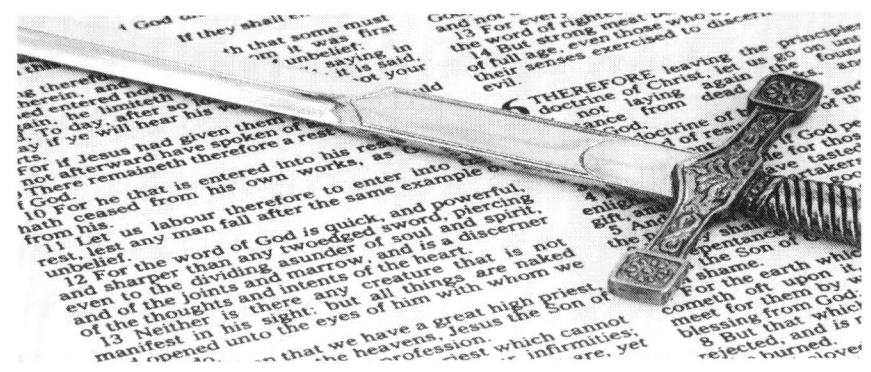

Chapter 11
The Strategy of Warfare

General Sun Tzu, a masterful military strategist taught weak soldiers how to become skillful warriors, the king's concubine how to become powerful warriors and through his sayings, he is still teaching individuals today how to become strong business leaders, military commanders and more. Even in the teachings of a masterful Chinese general, we can learn to be spiritual warriors, armed and ready for the battle that is being waged against us. We are not to be ignorant of Satan's devices, which means that we must be able to recognize his schemes, traps, and snares if we are to effectively watch, stand, fight and pray as commanded by our Commander In Chief, Christ Jesus.

Weak soldiers will mean defeat for any army no matter how large or small. Weak links can produce portals, gateways and doorways for the enemy to infiltrate. Every weak link in our lives must be strengthened.

Look at a comparison between Sun Tzu's teachings and the Word of God. Although Master Sun was an ancient Chinese warrior, his teachings contained spiritual undertones that I have found informative and worthy of including in this chapter. Our ability to grasp the strategies of spiritual warfare will determine how effective we are in the war. It is not our objective to wallow in the trenches of adversity year after year, our objective is to behead the enemy and stand armed and ready every time the enemy rears his demonic head.

Sun Tzu: Chapter 1: <u>Preliminary Reckoning</u>

Now, in war, besides stratagem and the situation, there are five indispensable matters. The first is call the **Way**; the second, Heaven; the third Earth; the fourth, the Leader; the fifth, Law.[6]

<u>Jesus, the Master:</u>

"Jesus said to him, "I am the way, and the truth, and the life; no one comes to the Father but through Me."

(John 14:6)

* * * * * * *

Sun Tzu: Chapter 1: <u>Preliminary Reckoning</u>

At the reckoning in the Sanctuary before fighting, victory is to the side that excels in the foregoing matters. They that have many of these will conquer; they that have few will not conquer; hopeless, indeed are they that have none.

The Word of God Teaches:

For whatsoever is born of God overcometh the world: and this is the **victory** that overcometh the world, even our faith. Who is he that overcometh the world, but he that believeth that Jesus is the Son of God? This is he that came by water and blood, even Jesus Christ; not by water only, but by water and blood. And it is the Spirit that beareth witness, because the Spirit is truth.

(1 John 5:4-6)

He that trusteth in his own heart is a fool: but whoso walketh wisely, he shall be delivered.

(Proverbs 28:26)

* * * * * * *

Sun Tzu: Chapter 2: Operations of War

Those who take advantage of the enemy should be **rewarded**.

The Word of God Teaches:

If your enemy is hungry, give him food to eat; if he is

thirsty, give him water to drink. In doing this, you will heap burning coals on his head, and the LORD will **reward** you.

(Proverbs 25:21-22)

* * * * * * *

Sun Tzu: Chapter 3: The Attack of Stratagem

To fight and conquer one hundred times is not the perfection of attainment, for the supreme art is to subdue the enemy without fighting.

The Word of God Teaches:

Wherefore take unto you the whole armour of God, that ye may be able to withstand in the evil day, and having done all, **to stand.**

(Ephesians 6:13)

Ye shall not need to fight in this battle: set yourselves, stand ye still, and see the salvation of the LORD with you, O Judah and Jerusalem: fear not, nor be dismayed;

tomorrow go out against them: for the LORD will be with you.

(Second Chronicles 20:17)

* * * * * * *

Sun Tzu: Chapter 3: The Attack of Stratagem

Therefore the master of war causes the enemy's forces to yield, but without fighting, he captures his fortress, but without besieging it; and without lengthy fighting takes the enemy's kingdom. Without tarnishing his weapons, he gains the complete advantage.

The Word of God Teaches:

Finally, my brethren, be strong in the Lord, and in the power of his might. Put on the whole armour of God that ye may be able to stand against the wiles of the devil. For we wrestle not against flesh and blood, but against principalities, against powers, against the rulers of the darkness of this world, against spiritual wickedness in high places. Wherefore take unto you the whole armour of God that ye may be able to withstand in the evil day, and having done all, to stand. Stand therefore, having your loins girt about with truth, and having on the breastplate of righteousness; And your feet shod with the preparation of the gospel of peace; Above all, taking the shield of faith, wherewith ye shall be able to quench all the fiery darts of the wicked. And take the helmet of salvation, and the sword of the Spirit, which is the word of God.

(Ephesians 6:10-17)

Sun Tzu: Chapter 3: The Attack of Stratagem

Now a prince may embarrass his army in three ways, namely:

Ignorant that the army in the field should not advance, to order it to go forward; or, ignorant that the army should not retreat, order it to retire.
- ➢ This is tying the army as with a string.

Ignorant of military affairs, to rule the armies in the same way as the state.

➢ This is to perplex the soldiers.

Ignorant of the situation of the army, to settle its dispositions.

➢ This is to fill the soldiers with distrust.

The Word of God Teaches:

Lest Satan should get an advantage of us: for we are not **ignorant** of his devices.

(2 Corinthians 2:11)

Neither give place to the devil.

(Ephesians 4:27)

He writes the same way in all his letters, speaking in them of these matters. His letters contain some things that are hard to understand, which **ignorant** and unstable people distort, as they do the other Scriptures, to their own destruction.

(2 Peter 3:16)

* * * * * * *

Sun Tzu: Chapter 4: <u>The Order of Battle</u>

The skillful leader is **steadfast** in the "Way"; upholds the Law, and thereby controls the issue.

<u>The Word of God Teaches:</u>

Therefore, my beloved brethren, be **steadfast**, immovable, always abounding in the work of the Lord, knowing that your toil is not in vain in the Lord. (1 Corinthians 15:58)

* * * * * * *

Sun Tzu: Chapter 5: <u>The Spirit of the Troops</u>

Moreover, in battle the enemy is engaged with the normal and defeated by the abnormal force.

The Word of God Teaches:

For the weapons of our warfare are not carnal, but mighty through God to the pulling down of strong holds.

(2 Corinthians 10:4)

But his bow abode in strength, and the arms of his hands were made strong by the hands of the mighty God of Jacob.

(Genesis 49:24)

When thou goest out to battle against thine enemies, and seest horses, and chariots, and a people more than thou, be not afraid of them: for the LORD thy God is with thee, which brought thee up out of the land of Egypt.

(Deuteronomy 20:1)

* * * * * * *

Sun Tzu: Chapter 5: The Spirit of the Troops

There are five notes; but by combinations, innumerable

harmonies are produced. There are but five colours; but if we mix them, the shades are infinite. There are five tastes, but if we mix them there are more flavors than the palate can distinguish.

The Word of God on the Five Fold Ministry:

And he gave some, apostles; and some, prophets; and some, evangelists; and some, pastors and teachers; For the perfecting of the saints, for the work of the ministry, for the edifying of the body of Christ.

(Ephesians 4:11-12)

* * * * * * *

Sun Tzu: Chapter 6: Emptiness and Strength

We become one body, the enemy being separated into ten parts. We attack the divided tens with the united one. We are many, the enemy is few, and in superiority of numbers there is economy of strength.

The Word of God Teaches:

And if one can overpower him who is alone, two can resist him. A cord of three *strands* is not quickly torn apart.

(Ecclesiastes 4:12)

Only that the generations of the children of Israel might know, to teach them war, at the least such as before knew nothing thereof.

(Judges 3:2)

Sun Tzu: Chapter 7: Battle Tactics

The general receives orders from his lord; assembles and settles harmony among the forces, and takes the field.

The Word of God Teaches:

And all this assembly shall know that the LORD saveth not with sword and spear: for the battle is the LORD'S and he will give you into our hands.   (1Samuel 17:47)

The noise of a multitude in the mountains, like as of a great people; a tumultuous noise of the kingdoms of nations gathered together: the LORD of hosts mustereth the host of the battle.

(Isaiah 13:4)

* * * * * * *

Sun Tzu: Chapter 7: <u>Battle Tactics</u>

There is nothing more difficult than battle tactics. Their difficulty lies in the calculation of time and distance, and the reversal of misfortune.

<u>The Word of God Teaches:</u>

To every thing there is a season, and a time to every purpose under the heaven. A time to love, and a time to hate; a time of war, and a time of peace.

(Ecclesiastes 3:8)

* * * * * * *

Sun Tzu: Chapter 7: <u>Battle Tactics</u>

A lack of ammunition, of supplies, or of stores, may

lead to disaster.

The Word of God Teaches:

The horse is prepared against the day of battle: but safety is of the LORD.

(Proverbs 21:31)

* * * * * * *

Sun Tzu: Chapter 7: Battle Tactics

He who is ignorant of mountain and forest, defile, and marsh, cannot lead an army.

The Word of God Teaches:

His watchmen are blind: they are all ignorant, they are all dumb dogs, they cannot bark; sleeping, lying down, loving to slumber.

(Isaiah 56:10)

For they being ignorant of God's righteousness, and going about to establish their own righteousness, have not submitted themselves unto the righteousness of

God.

(Romans 10:3)

* * * * * * *

Sun Tzu: Chapter 7: <u>Battle Tactics</u>

If the enemy offers an allurement, do not take it.

<u>The Word of God Teaches:</u>

But they that will be rich fall into temptation and a snare, and into many foolish and hurtful lusts, which drown men in destruction and perdition.

(1Timothy 6:9)

The fear of the LORD is a fountain of life, to depart from the snares of death.

(Proverbs 14:27)

* * * * * * *

Sun Tzu: Chapter 7: <u>Battle Tactics</u>

He who does not employ a guide, cannot gain advantage from the ground.

The Word of God Teaches:

Make plans by seeking advice; if you wage war, obtain guidance.

(Proverbs 20:18)

And he will appoint him captains over thousands, and captains over fifties; and will set them to ear his ground, and to reap his harvest, and to make his instruments of war, and instruments of his chariots.

(1 Samuel 8:12)

* * * * * * *

Sun Tzu: Chapter 8: The Nine Changes

The procedure of war is: the Leader, having received orders from his lord, assembles the armies.

The Word of God Teaches:

And when they shall blow with them, all the assembly shall assemble themselves to thee at the door of the tabernacle of the congregation. And if they blow but with one trumpet, then the princes, which are heads of the thousands of Israel, shall gather themselves unto thee. When ye blow an alarm, then the camps that lie on the east parts shall go forward. When ye blow an alarm the second time, then the camps that lie on the south side shall take their journey: they shall blow an alarm for their journeys. But when the congregation is to be gathered together, ye shall blow, but ye shall not sound an alarm. And the sons of Aaron, the priests, shall blow with the trumpets; and they shall be to you for an ordinance forever throughout your generations. And if ye go to war in your land against the enemy that oppresseth you, then ye shall blow an alarm with the trumpets; and ye shall be remembered before the LORD your God, and ye shall be saved from your enemies.

(Numbers 10:3-9)

Declare ye in Judah, and publish in Jerusalem; and say, Blow ye the trumpet in the land: cry, gather together, and say, Assemble yourselves, and let us go into the defenced cities. (Jeremiah 4:5)

Sun Tzu: Chapter 8: <u>The Nine Changes</u>

Generals must be on their guard against these five dangerous faults:

- Blind impetuosity, which leads to death.
- Over-cautiousness, which leads to capture.
- Quick temper, which brings insult.
- A too rigid propriety, which invites disgrace.
- Over-regard for the troops, which causes inconvenience.

<u>The Word of God Teaches:</u>

Not a novice, lest being lifted up with pride he fall into the condemnation of the devil.

(1Timothy 3:6)

These six things doth the LORD hate: yea, seven are an abomination unto him: A proud look, a lying tongue, and hands that shed innocent blood, A heart that deviseth wicked imaginations, feet that be swift in running to mischief, A false witness that speaketh lies, and he that soweth discord among brethren.

(Proverbs 6:16-19)

He that is of a proud heart stirreth up strife: but he that putteth his trust in the LORD shall be made fat.

(Proverbs 28:25)

* * * * * * *

Sun Tzu: Chapter 9: <u>Movement of Troops</u>

Numbers are no certain mark of strength.

<u>The Word of God Teaches:</u>

And the LORD said unto Gideon, The people that are with thee are too many for me to give the Midianites into their hands, lest Israel vaunt themselves against me, saying, Mine own hand hath saved me.

(Judges 7:2)

And the LORD said unto Gideon, By the three hundred men that lapped will I save you, and deliver the Midianites into thine hand: and let all the other people go every man unto his place.

(Judges 7:7)

* * * * * * *

Sun Tzu: Chapter 9: <u>Movement of Troops</u>

Even if incapable of headlong assault, if the forces were united, and the enemy's condition ascertained, victory is possible.

<u>The Word of God Teaches:</u>

But he stood in the midst of the ground, and defended it, and slew the Philistines: and the LORD wrought a great victory.

(2 Samuel 23:12)

* * * * * * *

Sun Tzu: Chapter <u>10: Ground</u>

The general who advances, from no thought of his own glory, retires, regardless of punishment; but only strives for the people's welfare, and his lord's advantage, is a treasure to the state.

The Word of God Teaches:

And he ordered the people, Advance! March around the city, with the armed guard going ahead of the ark of the LORD. (Joshua 6:7)

With your help I can advance against a troop; with my God I can scale a wall. As for God, his way is perfect; the word of the LORD is flawless. He is a shield for all who take refuge in him.

(2 Samuel 22:30)

Though an army besiege me, my heart will not fear; though war break out against me, even then will I be confident.

(Psalm 27:2-3)

****

Sun Tzu: Chapter 11: Nine Grounds

If there be a chance of victory, move; if there be no chance of success, stand fast.

The Word of God Teaches:

And the LORD said unto Moses, Wherefore criest thou unto me? speak unto the children of Israel, that they **go forward.**

(Exodus 14:15)

He will have no fear of bad news; his heart is **steadfast**, trusting in the LORD. His heart is secure, he will have no fear; in the end he will look in triumph on his foes.

(Psalm 112:7-8)

My heart is **steadfast**, O God, my heart is steadfast.

(Psalm 57:7)

****

Sun Tzu: Chapter 12: Assault By Fire

Regard well the developments that will certainly arise from the fire, and act upon them. When fire breaks out inside the enemy's camp, thrust upon him with all speed from without; but if his soldiers be quiet, wait; and do not attack.

The Word of God Teaches:

He hath cut off in his fierce anger all the horn of Israel: he hath drawn back his right hand from before the enemy, and he burned against Jacob like a flaming fire, which devoureth round about. He hath bent his bow like an enemy: he stood with his right hand as an adversary, and slew all that were pleasant to the eye in the tabernacle of the daughter of Zion: he poured out his fury like fire.

(Lamentations 2:3-4)

As you can see even the teachings of Sun Tzu can be useful when used for the right purpose. The word of God teaches that, the wealth of the wicked is laid up for the righteous. The wealth the Bible speaks of goes far beyond money. If we simply categorize wealth in terms of money, we have locked wealth in a box, hindering our advancement. We should be advancing for the Kingdom of God, not stagnant recycling the same messages and ideas year after year. Ever learning, but never prospering in the knowledge of spiritual matters.

Week after week singing, "I am on the battlefield for my Lord," and never fighting, standing or commanding. Attending church weekly defeated, dying and without answers to the devastating questions that pertain to spiritual warfare. It is time we stand and command, believe and achieve that which our Commander In Chief ordained before the foundation of the world.

Become a spiritual strategist, wielding the Word of God as your weapon of warfare. Through the comparisons of Sun Tzu's teachings, I believe it will show us that we can take an ancient Chinese perspective on war and use it in such a way that it gives glory to God and empowers believers to think higher and grow deeper.

The wealth of the wicked is not always in relation to money, land, property and the like, I believe one of the greatest wealth resources is intellectual property; the mind. The ability to use our greatest resource, gives us an advantage over the enemy and his devices. "Let this mind be in you, which was also in Christ Jesus" (Philippians 2:5). "And be not conformed to this world: but be ye transformed by the renewing of your mind, that ye may prove what is that good, and acceptable, and perfect, will of God" (Romans 12:2). "Wherefore gird up the loins of your mind, be sober, and hope to the end for the grace that is to be brought unto you at the revelation of Jesus Christ. As obedient children, not fashioning yourselves according to the former lusts in your ignorance: But as he which hath called you is holy, so be ye holy in all manner of conversation; Because it is written, Be ye holy; for I am holy" (1 Peter 1:13-18).

It is time to gird up our spiritual, mental and emotions loins and get ready for the battle. It is time to stand unmovable and unshakeable in the midst of the war.

The Art of Spiritual Warfare

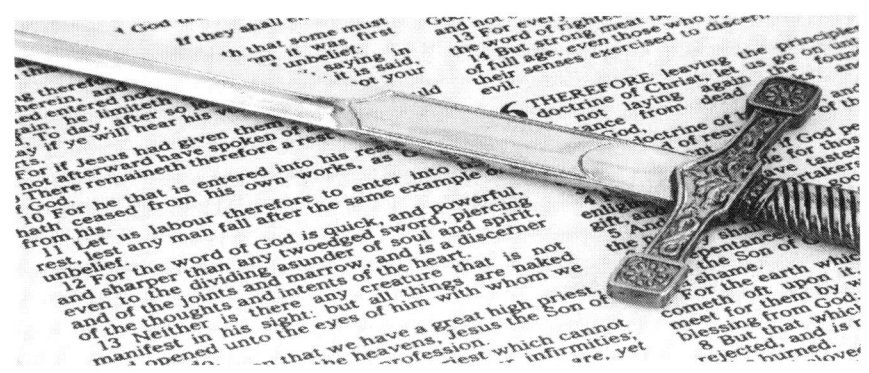

Chapter 12

Is Your House Clean?

Your weapons of warfare would not be complete without strategies that destroy the enemy that could be lurking in your camp. We have the authority to destroy his deceptive devices and we must be armed and ready to use them. There are steps you can take when you are faced with warfare in your home. Covering your home and your family is vital to the spiritual, physical and emotional heath of your family. Your home should be your sanctuary, your hiding place, your place of refuge.

What happens when the enemy infiltrates your home? Chaos, confusing, discord and more.

There are steps we have taken over the years to stand and defend our home. I pray these steps will help you stand and command during your time of warfare. I have taught these tactics to others in need of a strategy. "For this purpose the Son of God was manifested, that he might destroy the works of the devil" (1 John 3:8b).

STEPS TO GUARD YOUR HOME

1. **Clean your house.**
   - Remove objects that might be contaminating your home's atmosphere. (This will require prayer and a thorough spiritual inventory of your home).
   - Remove objects that open portals: Ouija boards, voodoo masks, tarot cards, psychic materials, astrology maps, pornography, drug paraphernalia.
   - Be mindful of video games that appear to be

- harmless fun, they can be a portal for demonic activity.

- Read Deuteronomy 7:25-26 & 1 Corinthians 10:19-20.

2. **Address any Achan's in your house.**
   - Read Joshua 7:11-26.
   - Remove stolen items regardless of how they came into your home.
   - Pray the *Shutting Demonic Doors Prayer.*

3. **Anoint your family.**
   - Yourself, spouse, children, grandchildren and animals.
   - Pray the *Prayer of Protection* while you are anointing.

4. **Anoint your house and land.**
   - Open the front and back doors.
   - Place a bible at each door.
   - Anoint each room including doorposts.
   - Anoint basements, attics, closets and garages.
   - Anoint the outside of your home.

- Pray the *Cleaning Your House Prayer while you are anointing each area.*
- Read Exodus 40:9.

5. **Stake your claim for the Lord** on your home, children, spouse, property, marriage, finances, health, family members, etc. Make a covenant (promise) that they are dedicated to the Lord. (Write out your declaration)

6. **Bathe yourself in Psalm 139**.
   Search me, O God, and know my heart: try me, and know my thoughts: And see if there be any wicked way in me, and lead me in the way everlasting.

7. **Take a spiritual inventory**. This is a part of your Psalm 139 prayer. Pray and ask the Lord to reveal:
   - Un-confessed sins of the past or present.
   - Strongholds.
   - Generational curses and soul ties.
   - Word curses prayed over you\your family.
   - Sins of pride, bitterness, resentment, un-forgiveness, etc.
   - Any participation in the occult.

- Pray the *Prayer of Deliverance*.

8. Ask the Lord to reveal any other portals or doors that have given the enemy access to you or your family.

9. **Guard your mind daily**. Be careful what you allow in your ear and eye gates. The enemy is waiting for an opportunity to infiltrate with weapons designed for your destruction. Pray the *Mind Cleansing Prayer.*

10. **Write out a declaration** for every area of your life and pray it daily. Cover the following areas in your declaration to God.
    - Your mind
    - Your heart
    - Your emotions
    - Your body
    - Your spirit
    - Your children or grandchildren
    - Your marriage
    - Your home, property, vehicles, etc
    - Your finances
    - Your health
    - Your family members
    - Your business or job
    - Your church and church family.

11. **Pray *The Armor of God Prayer* daily before you leave home.** Binding and loosing the enemy as commanded by the Word in Matthew 16:19: "And I will give unto thee the keys of the kingdom of heaven: and whatsoever thou shalt bind on earth shall be bound in heaven: and whatsoever thou shalt loose on earth shall be loosed in heaven."

12. **Read your word daily**.

13. **Covenant to increase your prayer life.** Start your day with prayer and end it with prayer. Read Psalm 63.

14. **Find a mid-week prayer service.** Prayer during your lunch period is a great way to set aside time for His presence. It is not the quantity of time you spend with Him, it is the quality of time. Seek the Lord for a prayer consecration: praying for example 6:00 a.m., 12:00 noon, 6:00 p.m. and midnight.

15. **Set aside quiet time with the Lord.** It does not matter whether it is early in the morning or late at night. Make time for His presence throughout your day. You will find it renewing and refreshing.

Spiritual warfare became a part of your life the moment you enlisted in the Army of the Lord. Since you are in the army, it is wise to learn the weapons of your warfare so that you will be able to stand in the midst of the battle.

Everytime the enemy launches an attack we should be ready with a counter attack. Ready, set, **FIRE!**

✥ **All the prayers listed are found in chapter 22.**

The Art of Spiritual Warfare

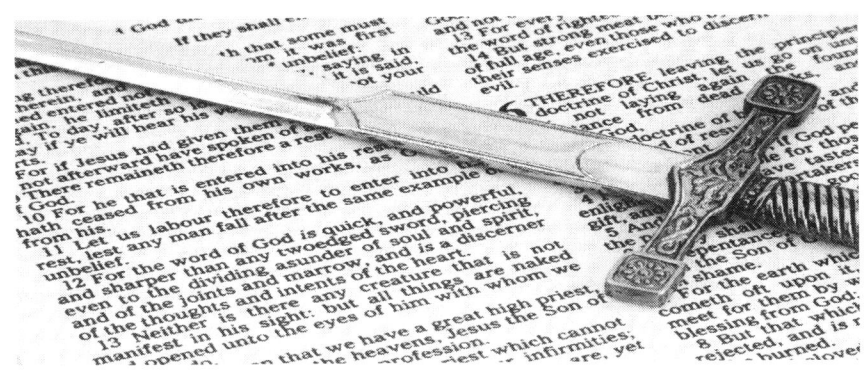

Chapter 13
Launching a Counter Attack

It is one thing to have the information needed to formulate the weapons of your warfare. It is an entirely different matter when it comes to using it. All the artillery in the world will not do the army any good if they do not know how to effectively us it.

The spiritual realm is a real unseen reality. Satan has

waged war against us. Along with his demonic forces, they are determined to destroy the soul of man and steal the glory from God. The war is for the possession of your soul, that is, your will, mind and emotions. It is not enough to believe IN God, we must BELIEVE GOD.

Satan is real and his kingdom is real. His destructive weapons are real and his hatred of mankind is certainly real. Therefore, it is vital that we arm ourselves against our deadliest enemy.

Just as Satan became twisted in his heart, he wants to deceive us in the same way. "How art thou fallen from heaven, O Lucifer, son of the morning! How art thou cut down to the ground, which didst weaken the nations! For thou hast said in thine heart, I will ascend into heaven, I will exalt my throne above the stars of God: I will sit also upon the mount of the congregation,

Launching a Counter Attack

in the sides of the north: I will ascend above the heights of the clouds: I will be like the most High. Yet thou shalt be brought down to hell, to the sides of the pit" (Isaiah 14:12-15). Knowing that Satan hates you and wants your destruction should move you to want to arm yourself. Let us discuss your weaponry and how to use it in the battle.

> And his fame went throughout all Syria: and they brought unto him all sick people that were taken with divers diseases and torments, and those, which were possessed with devils, and those, which were lunatic, and those that had the palsy; and he healed them.
> (Matthew 4:24)

Prayer

Prayer is one of the most powerful tools in your weaponry for effective spiritual warfare. No power of darkness can stand against the Word of God in the Name of Jesus and through the Blood of Jesus. Use your prayer language when you are in spiritual warfare. "In the same way the Spirit also helps our weakness; for we do not know how to pray as we should, but the

Spirit Himself intercedes for us with groanings too deep for words" (Romans 8:26).

Faith:

"But without faith it is impossible to please him: for he that cometh to God must believe that he is, and that he is a rewarder of them that diligently seek him" (Hebrews 11:6). Faith is to prayer what water is to the ocean. VITAL. Without faith, your prayers are useless. We must come to God believing by faith that we will receive according to His will. We receive our reward when we stand steadfast in faith believing in His promises. Faith is a valuable weapon against the tricks and wiles of the enemy. When Satan says you cannot, simply reply, "It Is Written that with God ALL things are possible." Remember, we walk by faith, and not by sight. You have the victory through Christ Jesus.

Fasting:

"Consecrate a fast, Proclaim a solemn assembly; Gather the elders and all the inhabitants of the land to the house of the LORD your God, And cry out to the LORD" (Joel 1:14).

Unfortunately, fasting has been mistaken for a way to get power from God to preach, teach and receive material things from His hand. If believers realized what great power and blessings they are missing, they would be happy to fast. Satan robs them of the great experience of fasting and he uses the misinterpretation and confusion surrounding fasting to rob Christians of one of the most remarkable experiences of their lives. Fasting accompanied by prayer makes it easier for us to delight ourselves in the Lord. We will not receive the full manifestation of God and all He has for us without a period of fasting and prayer. "We then, as workers together with him, beseech you also that ye receive not the grace of God in vain. (For he saith, I have heard thee in a time accepted, and in the day of salvation have I succoured thee: behold, now is the accepted time; behold, now is the day of salvation.) Giving no offence in any thing, that the ministry be not blamed: But in all things approving ourselves as the ministers of God, in much patience, in afflictions, in necessities, in distresses, in stripes, in imprisonments, in tumults, in labours, in watchings, in fastings" (2 Corinthians 6:1-5).

There are two important facts you should know about fasting. First, fasting wars against our members so that our senses, though perceptive, are subjected to the spiritual. Second, fasting is faith's greatest ally in the war against your flesh or sin nature.

The Word of God:

"In the beginning was the Word, and the Word was with God, and the Word was God. He was in the beginning with God" (John 1:1-2). "For the word of God is living and active and sharper than any two-edged sword, and piercing as far as the division of soul and spirit, of both joints and marrow, and able to judge the thoughts and intentions of the heart" (Hebrews 4:12). When the enemy attacks you, *speak the word*. When the demonic forces rage against you, *speak the word*. The Sword of the Spirit is living and active and fully capable to judge the thoughts, and intentions of the heart. Job 22:28 declares: "You will also decree a thing, and it will be established for you; And light will shine on your ways." Arm yourself with the Word of God and *speak those things...*

Blood of Jesus:

No power of darkness can stand against the Word of God, the Name of Jesus, and the Blood of Jesus Christ. They are powerful when wielded as part of our weaponry. "But now in Christ Jesus you who once were far away have been brought near through the blood of Christ" (Ephesians 2:13). "How much more, then, will the blood of Christ, who through the eternal Spirit offered himself unblemished to God, cleanse our consciences from acts that lead to death, so that we may serve the living God" (Hebrews 9:14)! "To him who loves us and has freed us from our sins by his blood" (Revelation 1:5). When you combine prayer, faith and the Blood of Jesus you have a weapon that makes the demons of darkness tremble and flee. Revelation 12:11 tells us that, "They overcame him by the blood of the Lamb, and by the word of their testimony."

Worship:

Worship is God's weapon of choice. Worship shifts the focus off us and onto God. When we are going through our trials and tribulations, our ability to worship will make all the difference in the world. It takes the focus off your problems, needs and wants and places the focus on Him. Jesus declared, "Yet a time is coming and has now come when the true worshipers will worship the Father in spirit and truth, for they are the kind of worshipers the Father seeks. God is spirit, and his worshipers must worship in spirit and in truth" (John 4:23-24).

Praise:

Praise is a potent weapon in your arsenal of spiritual warfare. "Praise be to the LORD my Rock, who trains my hands for war, my fingers for battle. He is my loving God and my fortress, my stronghold and my deliverer, my shield, in whom I take refuge, who subdues peoples under me" (Psalm 144:1-2). "To the end that my glory may sing praise to thee, and not be silent. O LORD my God, I will give thanks unto thee for ever" (Psalm 30:12). "Let them praise the name of the LORD: for his name alone is excellent; his glory is above the earth and heaven" (Psalm 148:13). God is worthy of our praise. He is our fortress, shield, strong tower, deliverer and more. He is our ALL. When we lift our hearts in praise we are acknowledging that He is ALL and in ALL.

Anointing:

It is the anointing that destroys the yokes of bondage. "And it shall come to pass in that day, that his burden shall be taken away from off thy shoulder, and his yoke from off thy neck, and the yoke shall be destroyed because of the anointing" (Isaiah 10:27).

Music

As a Prophetic Psalmist, I understand the importance of music as a weapon of warfare. "But now bring me a minstrel. And it came to pass, when the minstrel played, that the hand of the LORD came upon him" (2 Kings 3:15). "It came even to pass, as the trumpeters and singers were as one, to make one sound to be heard in praising and thanking the LORD; and when they lifted up their voice with the trumpets and cymbals and instruments of music, and praised the LORD, saying, For he is good; for his mercy endureth for ever: that then the house was filled with a cloud, even the house of the LORD" (2 Chronicles 5:13).

Binding and Loosing:

When you are praying a binding and loosing prayer incorporate your own requests and words into the prayer because it becomes personal to your specific needs. You have the keys, use them. "I will give you the keys of the kingdom of heaven; whatever you bind on earth will be bound in heaven, and whatever you loose on earth will be loosed in heaven" (Matthew 16:19).

The Word of God tells us in Second Corinthians 10:4-5: "For the weapons of our warfare are not carnal, but mighty through God to the pulling down of strong holds; Casting down imaginations, and every high thing that exalteth itself against the knowledge of God, and bringing into captivity every thought to the obedience of Christ." In other words, the weapons we fight with are not weapons of the world. They are not physical weapons of flesh and blood, instead they have divine power to overthrow and demolish strongholds. With them we have the ability to demolish arguments and every pretension that sets itself up against the knowledge of God. After which we then can lead every thought and purpose away captive to the obedience of Christ.

You possess an arsenal of weapons: prayer, faith, fasting, the Word of God, the blood of Jesus, worship, and praise, the anointing of God, music, and binding and loosing to war against the enemy. The Bibles tells us in Isaiah 54:17, "That no weapon formed against us shall prosper." It does not matter what the enemy throws at you, what matters is that you employ your weapons to war against him and you wield them with spiritual precision.

Remember, no weapon formed against you will prosper, and every tongue that rises against you in judgment the Lord will show to be in the wrong. Peace, righteousness, and security will triumph over the opposition of the enemy. This is the heritage of the servants of the Lord. Equip yourself with the weapons of your warfare and be prepared to expose the kingdom of darkness and destroy the works of the enemy.

The Art of Spiritual Warfare

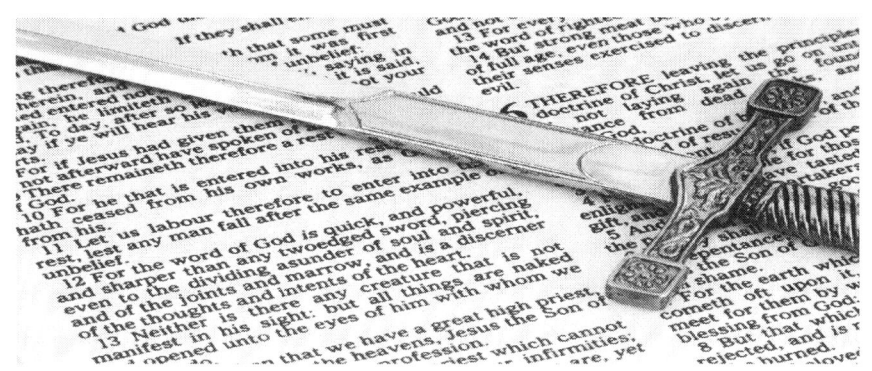

Chapter 14

Exposing Satan's Kingdom of Darkness

Some modern day churches will deny that there are demon possessed individuals. Although they do not deny demons exist, they deny that individuals can possess demons. Unfortunately, because of this position, demonic activity can have free reign in their churches. If you deny that the lights are out you will never flip the switch to turn them on. If you deny that demons exist you will never seek the truth in order to *"cast them out."*

While studying for this book, I noticed an important statement made by Jesus regarding demons, He said, *"cast them out."* We are not to make them comfortable, pacify them, or become acquainted with them in a friendly manner, we are to *"cast them out."* When a church or believer denies the existence of demons, they are denying a requirement for successful spiritual warfare.

Simply denying an enemy's existence does not cancel it's presence or power. We are warned not to be ignorant of Satan's devices and one of his best devices was to convince the world that he did not exist. If he does not exist, then his host of demons cannot exist. Jesus exposed a great deal about Satan and his demons during his ministry and we would be wise to allow the Holy Spirit to renew our mindset regarding this subject.

We cannot allow the enemy to continue to infiltrate the church and it's people with demonic activity.

In His ministry, Jesus went about setting the captives free. Free from the chains of bondage of the oppressor. "And He healed many who were ill with various diseases, and cast out many demons" (Mark 1:34). He delivered individuals from the "spirit of infirmity" in (Matthew 4:24; Matthew 8:16; Matthew 28; Matthew 9:33; Matthew 12:22; Matthew 15:22; Mark 1:27; Mark 3:11; Mark 5:13; Mark 7:26; Luke 4:33; Luke 6:18; Luke 7:21; Luke 8:2; Luke 10:20; and Luke 11:14).

One of the best examples of exposing Satan's kingdom of darkness can be found in the encounter Jesus had in the country of the Gadarenes with the demon-possessed men. In this encounter, Jesus teaches us several things about Satan and his host of demons.

"When He came to the other side into the country of the Gadarenes, two men who were demon-possessed met Him as they were coming out of the tombs. They were so extremely violent that no one could pass by that way. And they cried out, saying, "What business do we have with each other, Son of God? Have You come here to torment us before the time?" Now there was a herd of many swine feeding at a distance from them. The demons began to entreat Him, saying, "If You are going to cast us out, send us into the herd of swine." And He said to them, "Go!" And they came out and went into the swine, and the whole herd rushed down the steep bank into the sea and perished in the waters. The herdsmen ran away, and went to the city and reported everything, including what had happened to the demoniacs. And behold, the whole city came out to meet Jesus; and when they saw Him, they implored Him to leave their region"

(Matthew 8:28-34; Mark 5:1-17; Luke 8:26-37).

We can learn a great deal about demons from this incident. Knowledge is power, power to recognize and defeat the enemy that wages war against you. You cannot defeat an enemy if you have no knowledge of him.

Demons:
- Can cause people to be physically strong (v. 28).
- Can cause people to be violent (v. 28).
- Can live anywhere, under any conditions (v. 28).
- Will talk back to you (v. 29).
- Recognize Jesus as the Son of God (v. 29).
- Like physical bodies even animals (v. 31).
- Are numerous (Mark 5:9).
- Several can inhabit a human body (Mark 5:9).
- Are intelligent (Mark 5:10).
- Can be convincing and coherent (Mark 5:12).
- Must submit to Jesus (Luke 8:28).

- Can resist being cast out (Luke 8:28; Matt 8:29; Mark 5:7).
- Like Satan, they know the word of God.
- Once demons are cast out, they can return if your life is not covered through the word of God, prayer and obedience.

No one wants to be exposed, especially your enemies. Because Satan and his demonic forces know their end, they are steadily advancing in strength and presence to tear down and destroy as many souls as possible.

Jesus opened the door for us to recognize the enemy and his manipulative tactics. It is because of His ministry that we can understand and recognize the traps and snares of the enemy. "To keep Satan from getting the advantage over us; for we are not ignorant of his wiles and intentions" (2 Corinthians 2:11 AMP).

Jesus revealed His reasons for being here in Luke 4:18: "The Spirit of the Lord is upon me, because he hath anointed me to preach the gospel to the poor; he hath sent me to heal the brokenhearted, to preach deliverance to the captives, and recovering of sight to the blind, to set at liberty them that are bruised." It is vital that we understand why Jesus came to earth: "The reason the Son of God was made manifest (visible) was to undo (destroy, loosen, and dissolve) the works the devil [has done]" (1 John 3:8 emphasis added).

Jesus came to destroy the works of the devil. He did not come to pacify or compromise with the enemy, Jesus came to destroy his evil workings. This is the same commandment He gave his disciples in Matthew 10:1: "Jesus summoned His twelve disciples and gave them authority over unclean spirits, to cast them out, and to heal every kind of disease and every kind of sickness." Also in Mathew 10:8: "Heal the sick, raise the dead, cleanse the lepers, cast out demons. Freely you received, freely give." In Mark 6:7: "And He summoned the twelve and began to send them out in pairs, and gave them authority over the unclean spirits."

Finally, look at what He told the seventy in Luke 10:17-20:

> "The seventy returned with joy, saying, "Lord, even the demons are subject to us in Your name." And He said to them, "I was watching Satan fall from heaven like lightning. "Behold, I have given you authority to tread on serpents and scorpions, and over all the power of the enemy, and nothing will injure you. "Nevertheless do not rejoice in this, that the spirits are subject to you, but rejoice that your names are recorded in heaven."

The word ***authority*** stands out as one of the most powerful mandates Jesus could issue to his disciples, the seventy and to us. "I have given you **authority** to…" *Authority* means:

1. Right or power to enforce rules or give orders.
2. Somebody or something with official power.
3. Legitimate power.
4. Power to act on behalf of somebody else
5. Official permission to do something.
6. Obvious knowledge and experience. [7]

With authority [official permission from Jesus Christ] comes responsibility. The word *responsibility* means:
1. The state, fact, or position of being accountable to somebody or for something.
2. Authority to make decisions independently.[8]

When we accept the responsibility to carry out the assignments ordained by the Lord, we are accountable for giving Him our best. When we accept the assignment to engage the battle, we must be prepared to endure to the end. As soldiers we are given the power to act on behalf of Jesus Christ until His return. As a result, we are serving as His ambassadors (official representatives). When we accept the ambassadorship it means that we are required to be armed and ready to stand against the enemy. Jesus is saying, "I have given you authority _____(insert your name)_____ to tread on serpents and scorpions, and over all the power of the enemy, and nothing will injure you." Our Commander In Chief has issued a directive and it is our responsibility to follow his orders.

Mark 16:17-18 gives us additional clarity on our assignment: "And these signs shall follow them that believe; In my name shall they cast out evils; they shall speak with new tongues; They shall take up serpents; and if they drink any deadly thing, it shall not hurt them; they shall lay hands on the sick, and they shall recover."

Once again Jesus is giving us authority to do a work on

the earth in His Name. He also set the atmosphere to teach us about spiritual warfare and expose additional strategies to fight the enemy. Much is required of us because much is given to us, **His authority**.

> "From everyone who has been given much, much will be required; and to whom they entrusted much, of him they will ask all the more" (Luke 12:48 NASB).

Jesus taught us a great deal about the enemy and the artillery required for standing and fighting. He taught us elements vital for effective spiritual warfare.

He taught us to bind and loose.
"Or how can anyone enter the strong man's house and carry off his property, unless he first binds the strong man? And then he will plunder his house."

(Matthew 12:29)

"I will give you the keys of the kingdom of heaven; and whatever you bind on earth shall have been bound in heaven, and whatever you loose on earth shall have been loosed in heaven."

(Matthew 16:19)

"Truly I say to you, whatever you bind on earth shall have been bound in heaven; and whatever you loose on earth shall have been loosed in heaven."

(Matthew 18:18)

He taught us the enemy would not prevail.
"And I say also unto thee, That thou art Peter, and upon this rock I will build my church; and the gates of hell shall not prevail against it."

(Matthew 16:18)

He taught us that once a spirit is cast out it goes through dry places.

When the unclean spirit is gone out of a man, he walketh through dry places, seeking rest, and findeth none.

(Matthew 12:43)

He taught us that the house must be filled or demons will return with seven more wicked.

"When the unclean spirit is gone out of a man, he walketh through dry places, seeking rest, and findeth none. Then he saith, I will return into my house from whence I came out; and when he is come, he findeth it empty, swept, and garnished. Then goeth he, and taketh with himself seven other spirits more wicked than himself, and they enter in and dwell there: and the last state of that man is worse than the first."

(Luke 11:24-26)

He told us not to be deceived by the enemy.

"And he said, Take heed that ye be not deceived: for

many shall come in my name, saying, I am Christ; and the time draweth near: go ye not therefore after them."

(Luke 21:8)

He taught us to pray.

"Pray, then, in this way: 'Our Father who is in heaven, Hallowed be Your name. 'Your kingdom come. Your will be done, On earth as it is in heaven. 'Give us this day our daily bread. 'And forgive us our debts, as we also have forgiven our debtors. 'And do not lead us into temptation, but deliver us from evil. [For Yours is the kingdom and the power and the glory forever. Amen.]' "For if you forgive others for their transgressions, your heavenly Father will also forgive you. "But if you do not forgive others, then your Father will not forgive your transgressions."

(Matthew 6:9-15)

Jesus taught us about the weapons needed to fight the

powers of the enemy. If we take heed to His teachings we will be in position to take dominion and use the authority in the Name of Jesus. Do not be afraid to take authority because you have the keys of the Kingdom available to you. In Mathew 16:19 Jesus declares that "I will give you the keys of the kingdom of heaven; and whatever you bind on earth shall have been bound in heaven, and whatever you loose on earth shall have been loosed in heaven."

You have the authority, access it and know that as Philippians 2:10-11 declares, "At the name of Jesus every knee will bow, of those who are in heaven and on earth and under the earth." Jesus gave you first hand authority, it did not come by way of another individual. Therefore, it is yours and nothing and no one can stop you as long as you walk in His power.

The Art of Spiritual Warfare

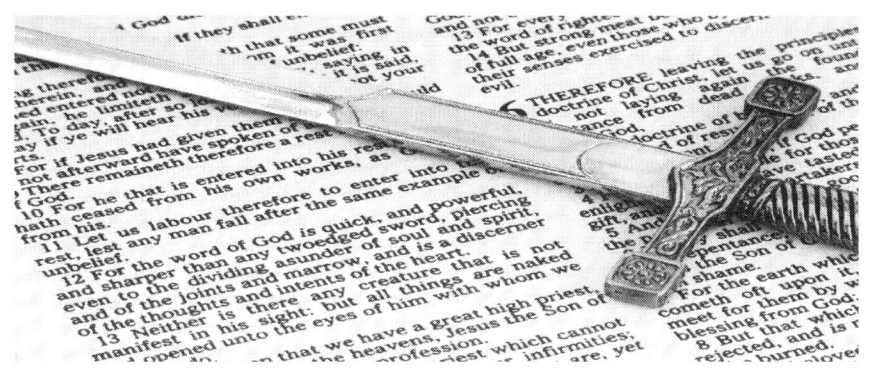

Chapter 15

Destroying the Works of the Enemy

A.W. Tozer wrote in his book, Warfare of the Spirit:

There are two spirits in the earth, the Spirit of God, and the spirit of Satan, and they are eternal enmity. Satan is aflame with desire for unlimited dominion over the human family; and whenever that evil ambition is challenged by the Spirit of God; he invariably retaliates with savage fury.

It is the Spirit of Christ in us that will draw Satan's fire. Satan will never cease to make war on the Man-Child, and the soul in which dwells the Spirit of Christ will continue to be the target for his attacks. In order to destroy the works of the enemy we must understand that the devil is wise and shrewdness is all that we may properly attribute to him, since sound moral judgment is an ingredient of wisdom and this the devil does not possess.[9]

This is a fact that we must embrace if we are to destroy the works of the devil. We must also understand that although he is shrewd, Satan does not have original thoughts or plans of his own. He is a copycat and he counterfeits the things of God.

Sun Tzu knew when to attack and when to stand, when to advance and when to withdraw. Unlike, Sun Tzu, Satan is not an astute strategist and is repeatedly defeated by God. Knowing this, it is important to stay in the Word of God, armed with the weapons of our warfare, which are not carnal, but mighty through God for the overthrow, and destruction of strongholds.

We must not forget that Satan is a formidable enemy and he is too cunning for us, but he is no match for the Almighty God. He is no match for the omnipotent (All-powerful One); omniscient (All knowing One); and omnipresent (The One who is everywhere) Lord of Hosts.

You will never defeat Satan with your worldly wisdom. Satan adapts well to the wisdom of this world and insinuates his input at every opportunity. Never attempt to defeat Satan with his own tactics, he will only be defeated with the Word of God; the blood of Jesus and the weapons of our warfare; prayer, faith, praise, worship and other spiritual weapons we have in our arsenal.

In order to destroy the works of the enemy that rage against your life, you must be armed and ready for the battle. Psalm 144:1 issues a battle cry that we must stand on: "Praise be to the LORD my Rock, who trains my hands for war, my fingers for battle." It is imperative that we are trained and equipped for the battle. When David was going into battle against the giant Goliath, Saul attempted to dress him in his battle array. David's response was, *it has not been proven (tested) and he took it off.* "Then Saul clothed David with his garments and put a bronze helmet on his head, and he clothed him with armor. David girded his sword over his armor and tried to walk, for he had not tested them. So David said to Saul, "I cannot go with these, for I have not tested them." And David took them off. (1 Samuel 17:38-39). You cannot defeat the enemy with weapons you have not tested.

Look at what happened to the Sons of Sceva when they

tried to cast out demons.

> "But also some of the Jewish exorcists, who went from place to place, attempted to name over those who had the evil spirits the name of the Lord Jesus, saying, "I adjure you by Jesus whom Paul preaches." Seven sons of one Sceva, a Jewish chief priest, were doing this. And the evil spirit answered and said to them, "I recognize Jesus, and I know about Paul, but who are you?" And the man, in whom was the evil spirit, leaped on them and subdued all of them and overpowered them, so that they fled out of that house naked and wounded" (Acts 19:13-16).

This is a perfect example of counterfeit ministers with a counterfeit anointing and counterfeit weapons, engaging a battle they were clearly not equipped to fight. What was missing?

1. Prayer
2. Firm knowledge of Jesus Christ
3. Personal relationship with Jesus Christ
4. Faith
5. The Blood of Jesus

The Sons of Sceva had no knowledge of the Name, the Cross-or the Blood. They said, *"In the name of Jesus, whom Paul preaches, I command you to come out."* This is a clear indication that they KNEW OF JESUS, but did not KNOW JESUS. They were attempting to cast out demons based on Paul's relationship with Jesus. They were defeated the moment they stepped into the house. Spiritual warfare is not based on your intellect, your degrees, your title or church affiliation. It is not based on your grandmother's relationship with Jesus. Effective spiritual warfare is based on your relationship with the Name, the Cross-and the Blood of Jesus - **Period**. Without a relationship with the Jesus, your efforts to walk in any area of ministry will fall into the, *I never knew you,* category. "Many will say to me in that day, Lord, Lord, have we not prophesied in thy name? And in thy name have cast out devils? And in thy name done many wonderful works? And then will I profess unto them, I never knew you: depart from me, ye that work iniquity" (Matthew 7:22-23).

The worst thing you can do is attempt to walk in a place you are not equipped. You cannot covet a person's anointing or gift simply because it looks glamorous or exciting. There is nothing exciting or glamorous about spiritual warfare. Never engage warfare simply because you see other ministers operating in the gift. In other words…

Don't Be a Modern Day Son of Sceva

There are many modern day Sons of Sceva in the church *"casting out demons"* they have no knowledge of, walking in bootleg authority, dressed in a counterfeit anointing, fighting with unproven weapons, possessing a knowledge **OF** Jesus Christ and having a form of godliness, but denying the power thereof (2 Timothy 3:5).

Their spiritual lives are torn and tattered, yet they proclaim to be spiritual warriors. They are plagued with the very demons they are attempting to cast out. It is impossible for a person with a "spirit of whoredom" to cast out the "spirit of whoredom." The Bible teaches us, "If a house is divided against itself, that house will not be able to stand. If Satan has risen up against himself and is divided, he cannot stand, but he is finished" (Mark 3:25-26). A house divided against itself cannot stand; it is the equivalent of trying to put out a grease fire with grease.

I have been in deliverance sessions with other deliverance ministers and we were on our spiritual post. Unfortunately, the altar workers astonished by true deliverance ministry, stood by like wide-eyed spectators. They were not efficient nor effective on the battlefield. This is an example of Christians who were not Christian Soldiers.

- **A word for leadership.** Make sure your altar workers are trained in deliverance ministry or explain the rules of engagement. A deliverance minister does not have time to stop and train your people. We also do not want to see them hurt physically, emotionally or spiritually.

Just as the Sons of Sceva were ill equipped for the battle, the modern day church might find itself in the same position. We need to suit up and maintain our spiritual post. We must be keenly aware of our spiritual surroundings; our prayer life, time spent in the Word of

God and our ability to rest in God. We must watch as well as pray and we must maintain a balance in every area of our lives; marriage, children; health, finances, etc. - give no place to the devil.

The best way to destroy the works of the devil is to be knowledgeable about what constitutes his "works." Recognizing portals, doors and gateways will go a long way in destroying his works. Time to close the portals of the enemy.

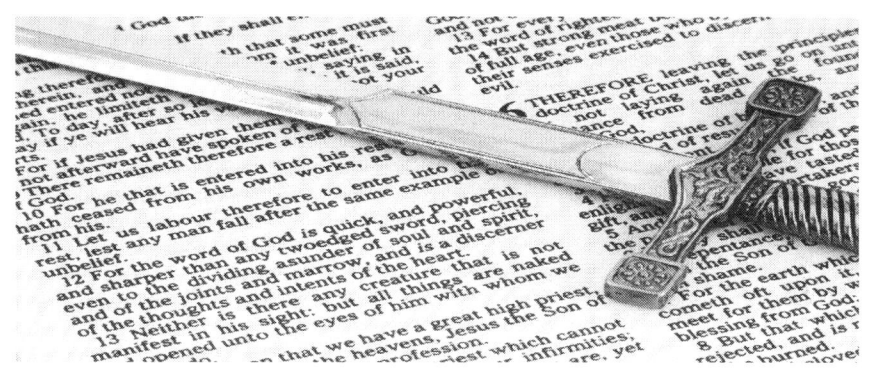

Chapter 16

Closing Portals, Doors and Gateways

What is a portal? A **portal** is:

1. A large or elaborate gate or entrance.
2. Any entrance to a place, or any means of access to something.

What is a door? A **door** is:

1. Movable panel at entrance
2. Gap forming entrance

What is a gateway? A **gateway** is:

1. Access point: a means of access to something

Have you ever asked yourself why the enemy keeps defeating you in specific areas? I am not speaking of the enemy occasionally bringing up your past situations; I am talking about areas that continually hinder your walk. Such as a person that gets off drugs, but finds himself, back in the drug house repeatedly with a crack pipe in his mouth. Alternatively, a man or woman who continually falls into adulterous affairs? The bible tells us that, "So if the Son makes you free, you will be free indeed" (John 8:36). A person that repeatedly returns to the drug house (vomit) might still have a portal, door or gateway open, which allows the enemy access.

An important fact about spiritual warfare and doors, portals or gateways is this: we determine how the

Closing Portals, Doors and Gateways

enemy, Satan operates in our lives. The Apostle Paul said, "Neither give place to the devil" in Ephesians 4:27. He was warning us to leave no room, toehold, doorway, portal or gateway in which Satan can have access. When we allow doors or cracks in our foundation, we are giving Satan a legal right to come against us. When we close the doors to Satan's attacks, we are shutting down his opportunity for advancement.

Sin is crouching at the door, ready to enter in. The Bible tells us Genesis 4:7 that sin was waiting for Cain. He had a choice to make, open the door to jealousy or keep moving in God's direction. Unfortunately, he chose what was behind the door called "sin" which led to the murder of his brother. "If you do well, will not your countenance be lifted up? And if you do not do well, sin is crouching at the door; and its desire is for you, but you must master it" (Genesis 4:7).

Sin is progressive and one open door leads to another and another. It is for this reason that we must find the open doors, close them and keep them closed through prayer, fasting and obedience to the Word of God. Otherwise, we will find ourselves in a room full of doors that lead to sin. What can open doors or allow them to remain open?

- Crisis or Trauma
- Curses **
- Generational curses (Exodus 20:5)**
- Ignorance of the Word of God
- Pride
- Disobedience
- Rebellion
- Un-forgiveness
- Fear, doubt or unbelief
- See Demon List in Appendix

The Word says that a **curse** without a cause cannot settle on a righteous person. Sin opens the door (primarily disobedience) for a curse to settle on a person. **Generational curses** are curses in which a parent or ancestral parent that we are in direct lineage of, has sinned and opened a door for it to be passed on from one generation to the next. Usually, there is some type of display or manifestation in the natural realm, indicating what the curse is, through a person's behavior. No matter how pronounced the manifestation is it needs to be dealt with through repentance. A curse without a cause cannot settle on righteous person or a person free of sin. Curses are clearly spoken of in the Bible and just because the Word tells us Jesus became a curse on a tree for us does not mean we cannot get a curse actively working in our lives. We get curses either through our sin or when we get into sin, a curse spoken of by others is attached to us after we sin, actively affecting us. We need to repent immediately! These things really do affect our thoughts and the thought processes of our mind more than we tend to realize. With generational curses, we also repent for our own sins and the sins of our ancestors. No matter the sin, and no matter the type of curse, we need to ask the Lord to take it and break it from us. Then we are appropriating and applying what Jesus did for us by going to the cross and becoming a curse for us.[10]

How do we close the doors and keep them closed? ARM YOURSELF with practical strategies for closing the doors and keeping them closed. We must have the necessary knowledge if we are to advance for the Kingdom of God, without it, we will be destroyed. We must be armed with knowledge of Satan and his devices. We cannot afford to wander through life ignorant and pretending the enemy does not exist. Likewise, we cannot be overly occupied with the enemy and forget the reason we stand - Jesus.

Hosea 4:6 warns us that, "People are destroyed from lack of knowledge." Proverb 29:1 also declares that, "A man who remains stiff-necked after many rebukes will suddenly be destroyed—without remedy."

Look at the following steps that will enable you to arm yourself and close doors to Satan's attacks. God has given us strategies in the Word to overcome the enemy's attacks; it is up to us to follow the directives of the Lord.

Steps to Arm Yourself and Close Doors

Step #1: Arm Yourself
- Know your enemy - II Corinthians 10:3-5
- Put on your armor - Ephesians 6:11-18
- Guard your mouth - Psalm 52:2; James 1:26; James 3:5, 1 Peter 3:10
- Guard Your mind - Philippians 2:5-12

Step #2: Search Your Heart
- Read Psalm 139
- Pray Psalm 51
- Confess all revealed sins

Step #3: Submit to God
- Read James 4:7
- Know the Truth - John 8:32

Step #4: Read your word
- Read II Timothy 2:5

Step #5: Stand in Faith
- Read Romans 10:17

- Read Hebrews 11:1

Step #6: Prayer
- Read Matthew 21:22; Mark 9:29; Mark 11:25
- Read Romans 12:12
- Read Philippians 4:6
- Read Colossians 4:2
- Read James 5:15-16
- Read 1 Peter 3:12

God wants us free from the bondages of the enemy. Walk out the steps to close the doors to Satan's attacks. It is time to put Matthew 18:18 into action as a part of your warfare strategy.

The Art of Spiritual Warfare

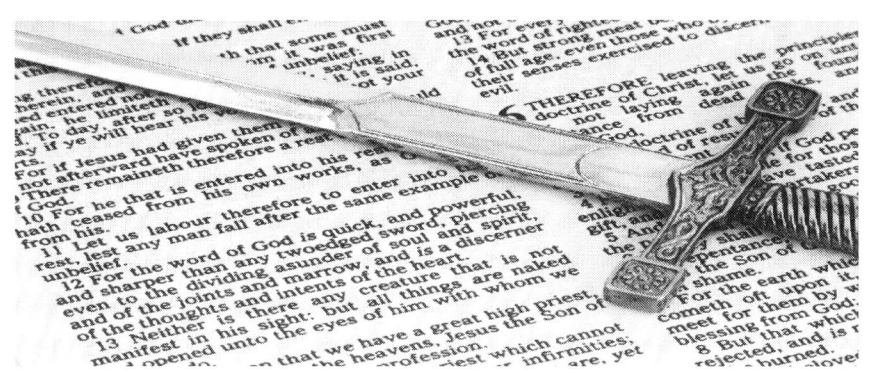

Chapter 17
The Warfare of Prayer

"Truly I say to you, whatever you bind on earth shall have been bound in heaven; and whatever you loose on earth shall have been loosed in heaven" (Matthew 18:18).

The Word of God is the cornerstone of our faith. The Sword of the Spirit is our offensive weapon for conquest. It is the weapon of our warfare that we wield to counter assaults from the enemy. Matthew 18:18 is our next step in closing the doors and keeping them closed.

When you come into the knowledge of binding and loosing based on Matthew 18:18, you will find a new level of spiritual warfare. The power of God in our lives increases as our faith increases. We must learn how to bind the enemy in the Name of Jesus and loose the Spirit of the Lord.

When we allow God to work in our lives we are opening a door that allows him full access to us, our family, finances, marriages, etc. God wants to be a repairer of the breaches in our lives and a restorer of the path in which we dwell.

The Lord wants to restore some desolate places in our lives because he desires that we are whole in every area. He wants us to bind all of Satan's demons, tormenting spirits and strongmen along with all principalities, powers, and rulers of wickedness in high places. He wants the doors closed and all willful sins destroyed.

Repentance and reverential fear of the Lord are vital to receiving your deliverance and keeping it. Psalm 66:18 and John 9:31 declare, "If I regard wickedness in my heart, The Lord will not hear; we know that God does not hear sinners; but if anyone is God-fearing and does His will, He hears him."

Prayer and fasting will reveal doors opened by sin. Confession and repentance will lead to God's voice being heard in your spiritual ear and His ear being attentive to your prayers. "If my people, which are called by my name, shall humble themselves, and pray, and seek my face, and turn from their wicked ways; then will I hear from heaven, and will forgive their sin, and will heal their land. Now mine eyes shall be open, and mine ears attent unto the prayer that is made in this place" (2 Chronicles 7:14). This will only be accomplished when we allow Him to reveal doors that need to be shut and open doors that He is ready to open in the spiritual and natural realms of our lives.

End this chapter with prayer. Have a pen and paper nearby so that you can write down any instructions you receive from the Lord. Ask Him to reveal any unconfessed sins, incomplete assignments or other areas that need addressing. Read and pray Psalm 51.

Ask the Lord to download His thoughts and plans, and pray for direction in each area He reveals. The Lord will give you clarity for each assignment and He does it with systematic precision. Keep a journal of your prayers. It will be a great blessing to you, your family members and others.

The Art of Spiritual Warfare

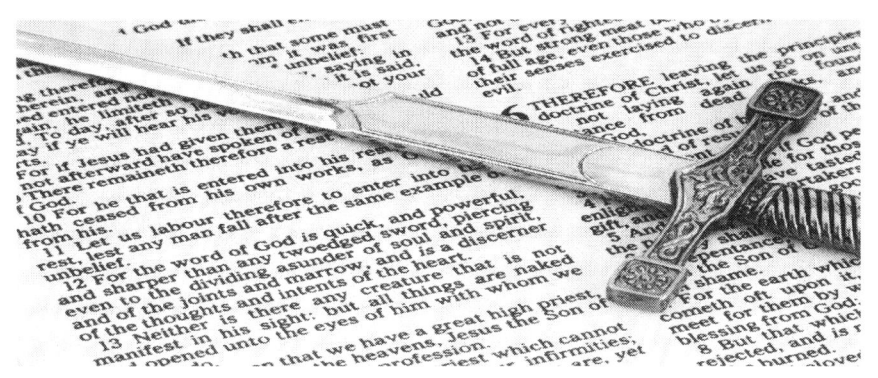

Chapter 18
The Importance of Prayer in Spiritual Warfare

The importance of prayer in spiritual warfare is clearly seen in Ephesians 6:18: "With all prayer and petition praying at all times." Also in 1 Thessalonians 5:17: "pray without ceasing." Without prayer, the battle is over before it begins. Prayer is the realm in which we fight. Prayer is extremely powerful and it endows us with the spiritual fortification, we need in the midst of the battle.

We engage the spirit realm through prayer. Our armor is useless without prayer because it is the key element that activates our armor. When we pray, things happen because the prayers of the righteous are powerful and effective. Prayer is also necessary because of spiritual resistance in the heavenly realm. Some things will not break out, break forth or break through without prayer.

In order to be a good contractor, you must learn to read blueprints. We must have a strong prayer life if we are going to be powerful and effective soldiers. Our prayers should be so authoritative and forceful that we literally shake the very foundations of hell.

A pastor from Nigeria came to inquire about purchasing our home and we began talking about prayer. He said,

The Importance of Prayer in Spiritual Warfare

"I must pray at least two hours each day because it takes me one hour just to get "me" out of the way." That was the fuel that ignited my heart to seek a deeper prayer life. I thought praying an hour was sufficient until I met a man that thought two hours was not enough. What would happen if we all possessed the same mindset and entered into prayer with the shear determination to shake the foundations of hell? I believe all of heaven would stand and take notice. The bible tells us in Matthew 11-12: "The kingdom of heaven has endured violent assault, and violent men seize it by force [as a precious prize—a share in the heavenly kingdom is sought with most ardent zeal and intense exertion] (AMP)." Imagine the deliverance and healings that would take place if we came together on one accord to assault the kingdom of Satan with our prayers. Marriages, finances, children, health, government and more would experience healing and lives would be changed.

You are a soldier in the army of the Lord and with that; come great responsibility to understand the importance of prayer and spiritual warfare. Properly armed with the weapons of warfare God has given us, we can launch an attack against the gates of hell. An attack that will leave his kingdom tattered and bruised. We cannot defeat the enemy on our own; it will take the power of God and the weapons of God to tear down the enemy of God. You possess weapons of authority and through prayer, you access that authority. Jesus gave you authority to carry out a work in the earth.

A good soldier is not a Sunday morning only soldier. A good soldier is a soldier - **everyday**. A powerful, formidable soldier is a heavily armed soldier - **everyday**. We are at war with our most dangerous enemy, and our responsibility is to watch, fight and pray. You cannot defeat the enemy with your own weapons; you must use the weapons of the Lord, because "greater is He who is in you than he who is in the world" (1 John 4:4).

Some of us have been down too long, it is time to pick up your weapons, arm yourself with the Word of God and advance for the victory through Christ Jesus.
Ready, set, WORSHIP!

The Art of Spiritual Warfare

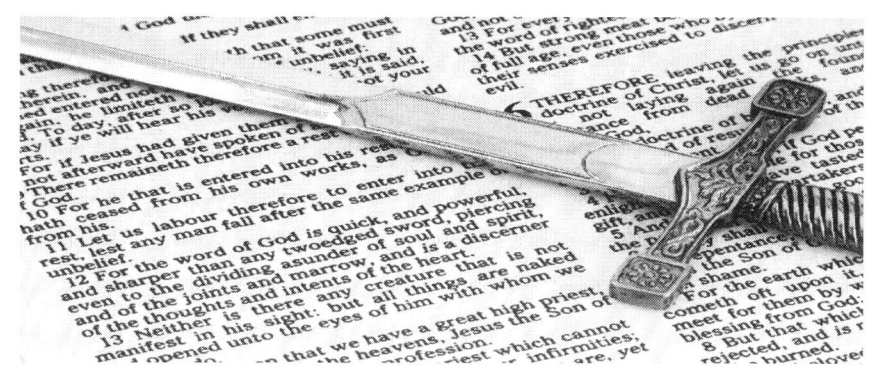

Chapter 19

The Enemy Hates Your Worship

Recently, during noonday prayer, there was a shift in the atmosphere that moved us from a warfare prayer position to a spirit of worship. When the shift happened, not only was there a breakthrough in the atmosphere, there was a breakthrough in me.

I turned off the microphone as I entered a place of worship I had not experienced in a while. There are times when we are so engaged in spiritual warfare that we fail to worship. Even in the midst of the battle, we must worship. Worship shifts the focus off us, off the warfare, off the cares of the world and totally onto God.

Satan wants the glory and worship for himself and he hates it when we worship God. I believe he especially hates it when we enter worship in the midst of our trials and adversities. It disturbs his strategy. His deceptive way of thinking:

- How can she worship when I unleashed financial hardships against her?
- How can he worship God when I ensnared his wife in adultery?
- Why would they worship God and their child was shot in a drive by shooting?
- Why would they worship God and they are facing unemployment?

- How can they worship and I sent sickness to their family?

- How can they worship God and I was allowed to come against them with ministry troubles?

When you realize you are wrestling with spiritual wickedness and not your circumstances - you will worship. If you want peace - worship.

The Lord has been there during every trial and tribulation in your life. He has been there through my five surgeries, he never left me. Even when I did not feel Him near, He was right there. He was:

- Strength when my finances were gone.
- Strength when I was in distress.
- My refuge from the storm.
- A shadow from the heat. [11]

God is everything to me. He is everything to everyone who trusts in Him. Whenever the terrible ones (Satan and his demonic forces) storm into the land, Our Lord, Jehovah Gibbor is always there lifting up a standard against the enemy. If God is all this to us, why not worship Him and cast your cares on Him?

Let's get back to my worship experience at the ministry. The worship was sweet; all around the room hungry worshippers fell like a gentle breeze. Individuals coming in for food or other items felt the "spirit of worship" and they too entered in. Worship in the midst of the war was akin to taking a sack of bricks off my back.

At one point during worship, a cry rose from my belly, unlike any sound I have ever heard or felt before. I equate it to a cry or shout similar to the shout in Joshua 6:5. I recall hearing cries coming from other areas in the room. The Commander of the Army of the Lord could only have orchestrated a synchronized shout. We were in different areas of the sanctuary - some were standing, others sitting or lying prostrate on the floor. Still, the cries of desperate and hungry worshippers went forth.

In our individual ways, we were in the midst of combat, but our shouts marked a shift in our warfare. "Have all the people give a loud shout, then the wall of the city (our warfare) will collapse and the people (worshippers) will go up, every man straight in" (Joshua 6:5 NIV paraphrased).

With our shouts of victory, a release went out into the atmosphere and walls collapsed as we stepped over and walked into victory. Prayer ushered in worship, worship ushered in a "shout" because the Lord gave us the city (our release).

Soldiers heavily armed with the weapon of worship can be a formidable warrior. The "shout" was an act of psychological warfare, which created panic and confusion in the enemy's camp. Why? Because in the midst of "going through" when we are on one accord as we "prayed through" to worship in the midst of the war.

Your shout of victory in the midst of warfare will confuse the enemy. When the enemy comes in like a flood, worship. When all hell breaks loose, worship. When you cannot see your way through, worship. Worship is God's weapon of choice because your focus is on Him and not your circumstances.

Remember, the weapons we fight with are not weapons of this world. Our weapons have divine power to demolish strongholds (2 Corinthians 10:4-5). We demolish, destroy, and annihilate any argument and every pretension that sets itself against the knowledge of God and we are to take captive every thought to make it obedient to Christ Jesus. Worship makes our thoughts obedient to Christ because the focus shifts off us and onto Christ.

There is a CD by the Watchmen Society entitled, "The Entermission." It contains an awesome song entitled, "Psalm 42 - I Yearn." It is an excellent song to usher you into the presence of the Lord. It plays in our prayer room twenty-four hours a day. It has been a blessing. My husband and I allow it to play throughout the house even when we are away. It is an atmosphere thing.

Soldiers of the Most High God, stand firm heavily armed, pray, fast, trust, believe and worship.

Here are words of worship:
- ❖ Yearn for God.
- ❖ Seek the face of God

- ❖ Give your all to God.
- ❖ Love the Lord your God.
- ❖ Worship God.

Having done all, STAND on the word and promises of God!

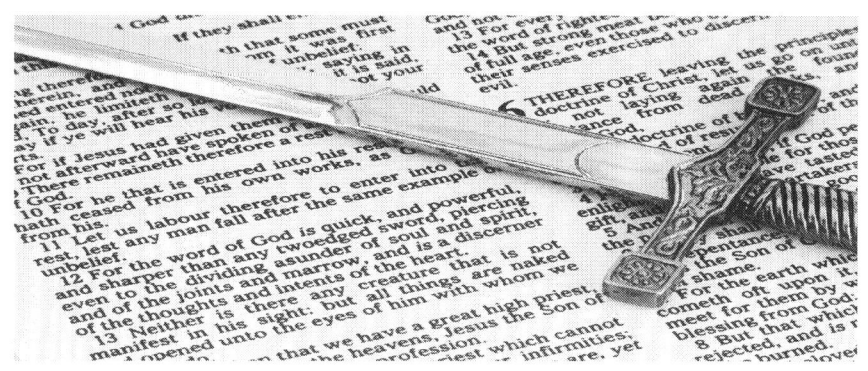

Chapter 20
Having Done All, To Stand

Therefore, take up the full armor of God,
so that you will be able to resist in the evil day, and
having done everything, to stand firm.
(Ephesians 6:13 NASB)

Therefore put on God's complete armor,
that you may be able to resist and stand your ground on
the evil day [of danger], and, having done all [the crisis
demands], to stand [firmly in your place].
(Ephesians 6:13 AMP)

Wherefore take unto you the whole armour of God that
ye may be able to withstand in the evil day, and having
done all, to stand.
(Ephesians 6:13 KJV)

A powerful soldier is a soldier who is heavily armed. Why? He is:

- Able to stand against all enemies.
- Able to withstand attacks against him.
- Able to quench the fiery darts of the enemy.

A powerful well-trained soldier knows three things:

I. He knows his armor.
    A. Defensive armor for protection:
- The helmet
- The girdle
- The breastplate
- The boots
- The shield

    B. Offensive armor for protection:
- Sword

The Christian soldier knows his armor:

- **The Belt of Truth (Ephesians 6:14).**

    When preparing for the battle the belt would be the first piece of protective equipment put on by the soldier. It clung closely to the soldier and shielded some of the most vulnerable areas of his body. The belt prepares one to be ready for action. The call to have "your loins girt about with truth" is a call to be *prepared.* [12]

- **The Breastplate of Righteousness (v. 14)**

    The Roman soldier would have fastened the breastplate around his chest.[13] The purpose was to protect the soldier's vital organs. Putting on the breastplate of righteousness means, believing in Jesus and His righteousness, not our own. Also, to stand firm against injustice and corruption. [14]

- **Feet prepared with the Gospel of Peace** (v. 15)
  Marching is an essential part of a soldier's life, and no soldier could march far without sturdy shoes. Even before the Roman era, the breaking of a soldier's shoe was a metaphor for weakness or defeat. The Gospel of Peace is the good news that we can have peace with God. The word peace means absence of worry. This peace is the confidence that God has everything under control. [15]

- **The Shield of faith (v. 16)**
  The shield of faith is the Christian's protection against temptation. Whenever we trust that God will provide everything we need, "the spiritual forces of evil" cannot tempt us with the lie that sin can provide a better life than God will.[16]

- **The Helmet of salvation (v. 17)**
  The helmet of salvation points to God's ultimate

victory over the forces of evil. Jesus' death on the cross and his resurrection from the dead provides all believers with freedom from the bondage of sin, and with eternal life with God in heaven. To put on the helmet of salvation is to accept that you are in a battle and will be persecuted for believing in Christ.[17]

- **Sword of the Spirit (v. 17)**

    The only offensive weapon mentioned in Ephesians chapter 6 is the sword. The belt, breastplate, shoes, shield, and helmet were not offensive; their purpose was defensive, to protect against the enemy. The sword was designed to defeat the enemy's plan and rescue lives. The "word of God" has several meanings (1) **The Gospel.** The message of salvation through Jesus Christ. (2) **The Bible.** When Jesus was tempted by the devil, he used the Bible verses to answer and the devil left him.[18]

II. He knows his enemy.

The Dake Annotated Reference Bible explains how the Lord will expose our enemies to us and show us how to overcome them:

> "Having laid before you your high calling and the great doctrines of the gospel. I will now show you the enemies that will oppose you and how you can overcome them."[19]

A mighty soldier knows his enemy and the traps, plans, and schemes used to deceive, entrap and enslave. The Lord will show you the enemies that will oppose you and how you can overcome and defeat them. The Lord will expose:

- Principalities
- Authorities
- World-rulers
- Spiritual Wickedness

- Anyone used as a puppet in the enemies plans against you.

✥ (See definitions in Chapter 7).

III. He trusts his Commander In Chief.

When you know and trust your Commander In Chief, you will obey His commands. Our Commander in Chief, Christ Jesus gives us twelve commands that will ensure we are prepared, enabled, and heavily armed with the armor of God - impenetrable and victorious.

When we trust our Commander In Chief, Jesus Christ, we will obey the twelve commands issued as our marching orders. They are based on Ephesians 6:10-18:

- Be strong in the Lord (v.10).
- Be strong in the power of his might (v.10).
- Put on the whole armour of God (v.11).
- Stand (v.11, 13, and 14).

- Have your loins girt with truth (v.14).
- Have on the breastplate of righteousness (v.14).
- Have your feet shod with the preparation of gospel of peace (v.15).
- Take the shield of faith (v.16).
- Take the helmet of salvation (v.17).
- Sword of the Spirit (v.17).
- Prayer and supplication in the Spirit (v.18).
- Watch with perseverance\supplication (v.18).

When you come into the knowledge of your armor, your enemy and your Commander, you are armed with comprehensive information that will ensure that you are effective and mighty through God, able to demolish strongholds. The only way to demolish strongholds is by knowing and walking in the truth.

Ephesians can be summed up in one word: **truth.** You now know the truth about your warfare, your armor, your enemy, your Commander and his commands. You shall know the truth and the truth shall set you free. It is vital that we stand free and knowing the Truth is what keeps us free. We must take the sure path based on Jeremiah 6:16 if we are to hold on to our freedom.

> Thus says the LORD, "Stand by the ways and see and ask for the ancient paths, Where the good way is, and walk in it; And you will find rest for your souls" (Jeremiah 6:16).

Pontius Pilate asked, "What is truth?" Truth is a never changing fact. When we stand on the Truth, we will not falter nor faint - we will stand. Truth begins and ends with the Word of God. Being armed with the Truth is your first position in the midst of the battle. Marching into a battle with misinformation is a sure road to defeat. There is only one Truth and God is that Truth. The Bible declares that God is Light and in Him is no darkness. "This is the message we have heard from Him and announce to you, that God is Light, and in Him there is no darkness at all" (1 John 1:5). This means there are no lies, tricks or deceptions when you walk in His truth. When all darkness has been dispelled, only Truth will remain. When truth is revealed, we can walk in the newness of life that comes to those who have a relationship with God through Jesus Christ. When truth is revealed through Jesus, we are then ready to engage the battle because your armor has been proven, tried and tested.

The spirit realm is a real place. Even though you do not see it, it is there. There is a war going on in the spiritual realm and it is a war for the souls of humanity. Those who live a lie will never defeat the enemy that is raging against them. They will continue to walk in defeat, always learning and never able to come to the knowledge of the truth.

Satan is out to dominate and destroy humanity and steal God's glory for himself. He who gets the victory gets the glory. Who is victorious in your life, You or Satan? Who is getting the glory from your life, God or Satan?

Do not buy the lie, Satan is already defeated, but we must walk it out and stand in the midst of the battle, in the midst of the flood, wind or rain. "When the enemy shall come in like a flood, the spirit of the LORD shall lift up a standard against him" (Isaiah 59:19). "And I say also unto thee…and upon this rock I will build my church; and the gates of hell shall not prevail against it" (Matthew 16:18). Again, Satan is already defeated; he will not prevail against us - the church.

Isaiah 54:17 declares, "No weapon that is formed against you shall prosper, and every tongue that shall rise against you in judgment you shall show to be in the wrong. This [peace, righteousness, security, triumph over opposition] is the heritage of the servants of the Lord [those in whom the ideal Servant of the Lord is reproduced]; this is the righteousness or the vindication which they obtain from Me [this is that which I impart to them as their justification], says the Lord" (AMP). No matter what trap, snare or weapon the enemy tries to use against you it will not prosper. The Lord did not say it would not form, He said it would not prosper. The Lord will allow some traps and snares to form in order to mature you. Remember His declaration in First Peter 1:7, "That the trial of your faith, being much more precious than of gold that perisheth, though it be tried with fire, might be found unto praise and honour and glory at the appearing of Jesus Christ." To whom is your trial precious? It is precious to the Lord. Why? Because through the fire, you were able to persevere. Perseverance is your steady and continued action or belief [your stand] despite difficulties or setbacks and in spite of the enemy coming in like a flood.

Regardless of sickness, death or disease - stand. Regardless of the enemy's constant attack against your mind - stand. Even though he launched a full frontal attack against your marriage, children and finances - stand unmovable and unshakable.

Notice that the Lord did not tell us to attack Satan. He said, having done all, to stand. Stand firm against the enemy because Jesus spoiled all Satan's principalities and powers, made a show of them openly, and triumphed over them. We are fighting for territory and the advancement of the Kingdom of God. It is our endurance of the trial by fire that brings God the glory. Ye though we walk through the valley of the shadow of…

Recently I was going through my valley of the shadow of, and the Lord gave me two scriptures to encourage me, and I feel led to share one of them with you. "We are troubled on every side, yet not distressed; we are perplexed, but not in despair; Persecuted, but not forsaken; cast down, but not destroyed" (2 Cor. 4:8-9).

- There will be times when it seems like the enemy has you surrounded on every side, but take heart, do not be distressed nor dismayed for the battle is not yours, but God's.
- There will be times when you feel perplexed by your situation, but do not despair; God is on your side.
- There will be times when you feel persecuted for no reason, but know that you are not forsaken. The Lord promised, He would never leave us for forsake us.
- There will be times when you feel that you have been cast down by the enemy, your friends or family, but take heart no evil shall befall you; neither shall any destruction come near you.

When you experience the presence of Jesus Christ, no sickness, trials, or disasters will cause your spiritual defeat. When your situation becomes unbearable and your assets are drained, God's resources are there to increase your faith, hope and strength. Romans 8:37 offers these words of encouragement, "In all these things we are more than conquerors through him who loved us." The Lord also gives us this promise, "Be strong and courageous. Do not be afraid or terrified because of them, for the LORD your God goes with you; he will never leave you nor forsake you" (Deuteronomy 31:6).

The word of God assures us that Satan is already defeated, therefore our mandate is to STAND, for the battle is not ours, but God's. Your military strategy is to recognize your enemy and fight the good fight of faith, holding fast to the Word of Truth, girded with the full armor of God and ready to engage the battle when warfare is presented.

The key is to have a relationship with our Heavenly Father, our Lord and Savior Jesus Christ and the Holy Spirit. They are truth and they are life. When we receive them into our hearts, everything will change, our character, our mindset, our perspective on life. Then we will not be so quick to believe a lie and fall into the traps and snares of the enemy.

Paul gives us a clear picture of what and whom we are fighting against in Ephesians 6:12.

> "For our struggle is not against flesh and blood, but against the rulers, against the powers, against the world forces of this darkness, against the spiritual forces of wickedness in the heavenly places" (Ephesians 6:12 NASB).

As we war against the enemy that rages against us, we must stand and as the old saints would say, "pray through." We must "pray through" our trials and tribulations if we are to break forth, breakout or breakthrough. As we "pray through" we must stand, press, keeping fighting until our victory is won. "For this purpose, the Son of God was manifested, that he might destroy the works of the devil" (1 John 3:8). STAND and watch the Son of God destroy the works of the devil in your life and having done all, stand with the Lord as your battle-ax.

The Art of Spiritual Warfare

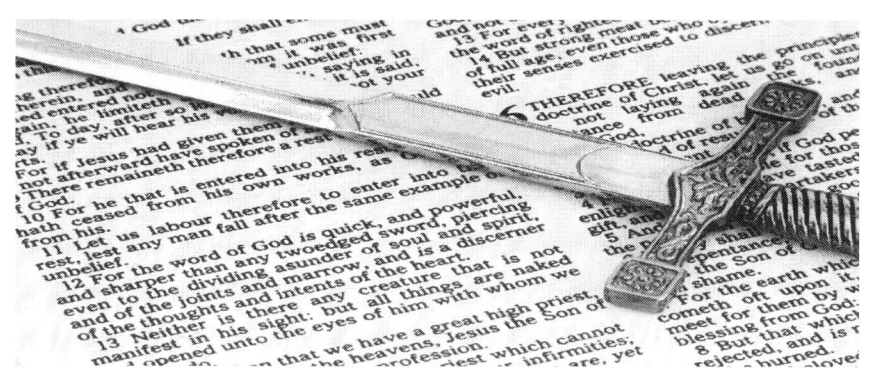

Chapter 21
The Lord is Your Battle Ax

*"Thou art my battle axe and
weapons of war." (Jeremiah 51:20a)*

The Lord is our battle-ax; He is the weapon of our warfare. Our struggle is not against flesh and blood, but against the rulers, against the authorities, against the powers of this dark world and against the spiritual forces of evil in the heavenly realms. The weapons we fight with are not weapons of this world. On the contrary, they have divine power to destroy strongholds. We must tear down arguments and every pretension that sets itself up against the knowledge of God, and we must take captive every thought to make it obedient to Christ.

The battle-ax, like our sword, must be wielded with spiritual precision, which means He must train our hands for war and our fingers for battle. Every warrior needs a strong fortress and for that reason, "God is our strong Fortress; He guides the blameless in His way and sets us free. He makes our feet like the hinds' [firm and able]; He sets us secure and confident upon the heights. He trains our hands for war, so that our arms can bend a bow of bronze. He has also given us the shield of His salvation; and His condescension and gentleness have made us great. He has enlarged our steps under us, so that our feet have not slipped (2 Samuel 22:33-37, paraphrased). The Lord is our Commander In Chief and we are fortified on every side of our fortress, armed and ready with the full armor of God. "Therefore put on the full armor of God, so that when the day of evil comes, you may be able to stand your ground, and after you have done everything, to stand. Stand firm then, with the belt of truth buckled around your waist, with the breastplate of righteousness in place, and with your feet fitted with the readiness that comes from the gospel of peace. In addition to all this, take up the shield of faith, with which you can extinguish all the flaming arrows of the evil one. Take the helmet of salvation and the sword of the Spirit, which is the word of God. And pray in the Spirit on all occasions with all kinds of prayers and requests. With this in mind, be alert and always keep on praying for all the saints (Ephesians 6:13-18).

Here is a Battle Cry Prayer to wield as you are waging war in the spirit realm. It is based on Jeremiah chapter

51. Pray it over your life, your family, your employment, your business, our government and our churches or ministries.

Heavenly Father, In the Name and authority of Jesus Christ and by the power of His shed Blood, you are my battle-axe and my weapon of war.

With you, O Lord, I shatter infirmities, sickness, disease and death.

With you, I shatter fear, rejection, pride, unbelief, doubt, bitterness, torment, anger, confusion and unforgiveness, jealous and envy.

With you, I shatter poverty, lack, debt and financial destruction.

With you, I shatter spiritual and physical abortions and miscarriages.

With you, I shatter abuse, lust, rape, and incest.

With you, I shatter spousal abuse, adultery, fornication, divorce and separation.

With you, I shatter compromise, laziness and slothfulness.

With you, I shatter addictions, perversions, obsessions, cravings and lust.

With you I shatter chains, cords, shackles, spells, and curses over my life and my family.

With you, I shatter counterfeit shepherds and itching eared flocks.

With you, I shatter false prophets, false teachers, false anointing and temple harlots.

With you, I shatter the Spirit of Competition, the Spirit of Jezebel, the Spirit of Absalom, the Spirit of Ananias & Sapphira, the Spirit of Leviathan, the Spirit of Belial, the Spirit of Carnality, the Spirit of Fear, the Spirit of Compromise, the Spirit of Jealousy, the Spirit of Pride, and the Spirit of Anti-Christ, that are trying to infiltrate the church.

With you, I shatter false anointings and release Your anointing to destroy the yokes of bondage.

With you I shatter all chains, cords, shackles, spells, and curses over my church.

With you, I shatter corrupt city, state and federal governments and governmental officials.

With you, I shatter all chains, cords, shackles, spells, and curses over our city, state and federal government.

Through the Blood of Jesus, I loose myself, my family, my church, my city, my state and all governmental agencies from the bondages of the enemy and command the spirits that once controlled these areas back to the pits of hell, never to return. In the name of Jesus.

Lord, I thank you for setting us free from every curse and every spirit that has operated in our lives, our *churches and our government. I thank you that we are free to love, obey and worship you. In the Name of Jesus.*

We will be still, and know that You are God; You will be exalted among the nations, You will be exalted in the earth" (Psalm 46:10). In the Name of Jesus. Amen.

As you take up the full armor of God, it is imperative that you are armed and ready for the battle that is being waged against you. A heavily armed soldier is one who able to stand against the captain of evil and his demonic forces; withstand all attacks by the enemy; and able to quench the darts and missiles of the enemy.

I pray that this warfare-training manual has equipped you to stand in the midst of the battle and endure the torrential rains of the flood that rages against us. "When the enemy shall come in like a flood, the spirit of the LORD shall lift up a standard against him"

(Isaiah 59:19). The Lord has lifted the standard and as you raise your hands in complete surrender to His purpose and plan, you are also raising your hands and heart in victory.

Soldiers of the Lord Christ Jesus, arise, and put on your armor. Now that you know the tactics, tricks, traps and deceptions of the enemy, and you are armed with strategies for effective spiritual warfare, stand strong in the strength, which God supplies through His Son, Jesus. As you go from strength to strength, watch, fight and pray! You now know your enemy, and you are endowed with and clothed with the armor of God. You are impenetrable, indestructible and victorious. "Therefore put on the full armor of God, so that when the day of evil comes, you may be able to stand your ground, and after you have done everything, **to stand**" (Ephesians 6:13).

The Lord is Your Battle Ax

Soldiers of Christ, arise, and put your armor on,
Strong in the strength which God supplies
through his Eternal Son.
Strong in the Lord of Hosts,
and in His mighty power.
Who in the strength of Jesus trusts is more
than a conqueror.
Leave no unguarded place,
no weakness of the soul,
Take every virtue, every grace,
and fortify the whole.
Indissolubly joined, to battle all proceed;
But arm yourselves with all the mind that was in Christ,
Your Head.

Pray without ceasing, pray, your Captain gives the
word; His summons cheerfully,
obey and call upon the Lord.

To God your every want in instant prayer display,
Pray always; pray and never faint;
pray without ceasing, pray!

From strength to strength, go on,
wrestle, fight and pray!
Tread all the powers of darkness down and
win the well-fought day.

Still let the Spirit cry in all His soldiers, Come!"
Till Christ the Lord descends from on high
and takes the conquerors home.[20]
Bobbie Saulsberry

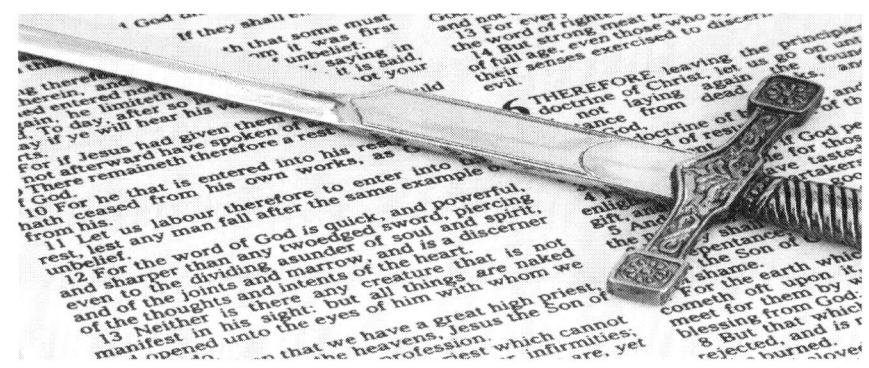

Chapter 22

Declarative Prayers

Binding and Loosing Demonic Spirits
Armor of God Prayer
Spiritual Warfare Prayer
Angels of Protection Prayer
Bind My Mind to the Will of God
Blood of Jesus Covering
Cleansing Your Home Prayer
Prayer of Deliverance
Shattering Strongholds
Cleansing Church or Ministry

Binding & Loosing Demonic Spirits

Heavenly Father, I thank you that whatever I bind on earth shall be bound in Heaven and whatsoever loose on earth shall be loosed in heaven.

In the Name of the Lord Jesus, I bind all of Satan's evil, wicked, demon, lying and tormenting spirits and strongmen along with all evil principalities, powers and rulers of wickedness in high places; including all their works, roots, fruits, tentacles and links including any spirits and strongmen of doubt, unbelief, leviathan, pride, anger, rage, strife, deception, self-deception, delusion unforgiveness, witchcraft, and willful sins, _____, _____, _____.

I bind and loose all these demonic spirits and strongmen from me, from everyone that I pray for today, from every organ in our bodies, from every cell in our bodies, from every gland, muscle, ligament and bone in our bodies, from our homes, properties, marriages, cars, trucks, businesses, ministries, work places, finances, pets and I loose them back into the pits of hell never to return and I bind them and command them to stay there, in the Name of Jesus. I place the Blood of Jesus Christ between us.

Heavenly Father, in the Name of Jesus, it is written in Psalms 91, and Matthew 6 that you are my deliverer and I ask that You give me total deliverance, total freedom, total liberty and total salvation from all evil, wicked, demon, lying, perverse, unclean, foul, demonic spirits, strongmen, and their messengers, and from all sicknesses, diseases, infirmities, afflictions, infections, viruses, inflammation, disorders of any kind, cancers, tumors, spasms, legions, or cysts in any parts of my body. Lord, I ask you to give my home, cars, trucks, offices, businesses, finances, ministries, properties and pets: total deliverance, liberty, and freedom from all evil, wicked, lying, perverse and unclean spirits in the Name of Jesus. I thank you for giving me this deliverance, freedom, liberty and salvation from all these things in the name of the Lord Jesus Christ. Heavenly Father, I ask You to give me divine healing, divine health and the manifestation of every miracle and every healing that you have ever given according to John 16:23. May these deliverances be used to glorify You. In the Name of Jesus Christ, I command my mind, will, and emotions to submit to the obedience of Christ in me. To God be the glory. Amen!

Space for Journaling

Armor of God

Heavenly Father, I am thankful for Your mighty armor that You have provided for me. I put on the full armor of God; the Helmet of Salvation; the Breastplate of Righteousness; the Girdle of Truth; Sandals of Peace; the Shield of Faith which protects me from all the fiery darts of the enemy; and I pick up the Sword of the Spirit, the Word of God that I choose to use against all the forces of evil in my life. I ask You Lord according to John 14:13-14, to be my Guard and Shield. Take me in the cleft of the Rock and underneath Your Mighty Wings according to Psalm 91. I put Your Armor on me and live and pray in complete dependence upon You; and pray in the Spirit at all times and on all occasions. In the Name of Jesus Name. Amen (Ephesians 6:10-18).

Space for Journaling

Spiritual Warfare Prayer

Heavenly Father, I come to now in the Name of my Lord and Savior Jesus Christ. Father, I ask you to forgive me for all of my sins, iniquities, trespasses, transgressions, and sins of commission, sins of omission and especially any sins of: _____, _____, and _____

And any unknown sins according to Psalms 19:12. Cover them with the blood of the Lord Jesus Christ, and cleanse me of all unrighteousness according to Your Word in 1 John 1:9 and John 14:14, in Jesus Christ's Holy Name.

Heavenly Father, I thank you that no weapon formed against me shall prosper. I thank you that every tongue and every word that rises against me in judgment; you shall condemn. I thank you that this is the heritage of the servants of the Lord, and our righteousness is from you according to Isaiah 54:17.

I thank you that it is written "for the weapons of our warfare are not carnal, but mighty through God to the pulling down of strongholds; Casting down imaginations, and every high thing that exalts itself against the knowledge of God, and bringing into captivity every thought to the obedience of Christ according to 2 Corinthians 10:4-5.

Father, In the Name of Jesus, I pull down every demonic stronghold of (_____name them if you know them - doubt, confusion, fear, lust etc.) that I have in my mind. I pull down and cast them back into the pits of hell in the Name of Jesus. I pull down every vain imagination in me. I pull them down and cast them back into the pits of hell in the name of Jesus. I pull down every high thought in me that exalts itself against the knowledge of God. I pull them down and cast them back into the pits of hell in the Name of Jesus. I bring every thought captive to the obedience of Christ Jesus according to 1 Corinthians 10:3-6. Lord Jesus, I thank

Declarative Prayers

you that "the yoke will be destroyed because of the anointing oil," according to Isaiah 10:27. Heavenly Father, I ask You now to cause Your anointing to break and destroy any yokes of bondage including (name them: fear, doubt, lust, drug abuse, sexual impurity, etc.) along with all of their works, roots, fruits, tentacles and links that are in my life. Father, I ask You to give me deliverance and freedom from all these bondages in the Name of Jesus according to John 16:23.

Heavenly Father, I ask You according John 14:14 to loose Your angels in great abundance in my presence, and into my home, cars, trucks, land, properties, buildings, and work places, in great abundance, protect us, guard us, and to force out, drive out, and cleanse out all evil, wicked demon and tormenting spirits from my presence, and our homes, cars, trucks, land, properties, animals, and work places and send them to the pits of hell never to return, in Christ Jesus' Holy Name.

Heavenly Father, I pray Psalms 35:1-8 over my family and myself. *"Plead my cause, O LORD, with them that strive with me: fight against them that fight against me. Take hold of shield and buckler, and stand up for mine help. Draw out also the spear, and stop the way against them that persecute me: say unto my soul, I am thy salvation. Let them be confounded and put to shame that seek after my soul: let them be turned back and brought to confusion that devise my hurt. Let them be as chaff before the wind: and let the angel of the LORD chase them. Let their way be dark and slippery: and let the angel of the LORD persecute them. For without cause have they hid for me their net in a pit, which without cause they have digged for my soul. Let destruction come upon him unawares; and let the net that he hath hid catch himself: Into that, very destruction let him fall.*

Hear my cry, O God, attend to my prayer. From the end of the earth I will cry unto You, when my heart is overwhelmed, lead me to the rock that is higher than I. For You have been a shelter for me. A strong tower from the enemy. I will abide in Your tabernacle forever, I will trust in the shelter of Your wings. For You, O God, have heard my vows; You have given me the heritage of those who fear Your name. I ask You to let me abide with You forever and prepare mercy and truth, which may preserve me. So I will sing praise to Your Name forever, that I may daily perform my vows according to Psalm 61.

Father, in You, O Lord I put my trust; let me never be ashamed; Deliver me in Your righteousness. Bow down Your ear to me, deliver me speedily; Be my rock of refuge, a fortress of defense to save me. For You are my rock and my fortress. Therefore, for Your Name's sake, lead me and guide me. Pull me out of the net that they have secretly laid for me. For you are my strength. Into You hand I commit my spirit; Redeem me, O Lord of truth, I have hated those who regard useless idols;

but I trust in You, Heavenly Father. I will be glad and rejoice in Your mercy, for you have considered my trouble; You have known my soul in adversities, and You have not shut me up into the hand of the enemy; You have set my feet in a wide place. Have mercy on me, O Lord, for I am in trouble according to Psalm 31:1-9.

My Father, I thank you that it is written in Psalms 32; Blessed is he whose transgression is forgiven, whose sin is covered. Blessed is the man to whom the Lord does not impute iniquity, and in whose spirit there is no deceit. I have acknowledged my sin to You, and my iniquity I have not hidden. I said "I will confess my transgressions to the Lord," and You forgave the iniquity of my sin. For this cause, everyone who is godly shall pray to You in a time when You may be found; surely, in a flood of great waters they shall not come near me. You are my hiding place, my resting place; You shall preserve me from trouble; You shall surround me with songs of deliverance. I thank You for instructing and teaching me in the way I should go and guiding me with Your eyes. Heavenly Father, In the Name of Jesus, I thank You "for when the enemy shall come in like a flood Your Holy Spirit will lift up a standard against him" according to Isaiah 59:19. I ask You in the Name of Jesus to nullify, dismantle, cancel, stop, annihilate, all works of darkness, which are designed to hinder, prevent, deny, or delay Your original plans and purposes for my life. Lord Jesus, thank You for redeeming me from the curse according to Galatians 3:13; "Christ redeemed us from the curse of the Law, having become a curse for us." Father God, In the Name of Jesus, thank you for saving all members of my household according to Acts 16:31; "Believe on the Lord Jesus Christ, and you will be saved, you and your household." In the Name of Jesus Christ. Amen.

Space for Journaling

Angels for Protection

Heavenly Father, In the Name of Jesus, according to John 14:14 I ask You Lord Jesus to loose Your angels in great abundance in my presence, the presence of everyone I pray for today and into our homes, cars, trucks, lands, properties, buildings, and work places to protect us, guard us, and to force out, drive out and cleanse out all evil, wicked, demon, and tormenting spirits from our presence, and our homes, cars, trucks land, properties, buildings, and work places and force them into the pits of hell and any replacement thereof, and they can not return to us. Lord Jesus, I ask You to create a hedge of protection of angels around each of our minds, and loose Your Mighty and Warring angels around each of us, our homes, cars, trucks, land, properties, buildings, animals and work places to protect us from the enemy. I ask you to do this according to John 14:14, *"If you ask Me anything in My name, I will do it.* In Jesus Holy Name, amen!

Space for Journaling

Bind My Mind to the Will of God

Heavenly Father, In the Name and authority of Jesus Christ and by the power of His shed Blood, I come to You now as I bind my mind to the will of God, I bind _____ mind to the will of God in the Name of Jesus Christ. Romans 12:2 tells us to not conform any longer to the pattern of this world, but be transformed by the renewing of my mind. Then I will be able to test and approve what God's will is—his good, pleasing and perfect will. Heavenly Father, in the name of Jesus, I ask you to transform my mind into Your mind. In the Name of Jesus, I pray with thanksgiving. Amen.

Space for Journaling

Blood of Jesus Covering

Heavenly Father, In the Name and authority of Jesus Christ and by the power of His shed Blood, I plead the Blood of Jesus, the Blood Covenant, and Psalms 91 over, through, around and about me, my spirit, mind, will, emotions, ego, sex drive, imagination, thoughts, and all subconscious areas and physical beings, all spiritual and natural doors and openings coming into my life and properties, the atmosphere above, around about me and my homes, cars, lands, properties, animals, vehicles, and work places, in Jesus' Name. Amen!

Space for Journaling

Cleansing Your Home

Heavenly Father, I come to You now in the Name of my Lord and Savior, Jesus Christ. Heavenly Father, in the Name and Authority of the Lord Jesus Christ and by the power of His Shed Blood, I now renounce all opportunities for ground held by Satan's wicked demons in relation to our home and property. I bind with chains and fetters of iron all wicked spirits and their schemes and assignments, against this home and property. I ask my Lord Jesus to evict them from this home and property, with any controlling powers of darkness, and to send them where they may never control or harm any person again. Heavenly Father, in the Name and authority of Jesus and by the power of His shed Blood, I now renounce all past use of this property for false religions, occult practices, divination, magic, sorcery, witchcraft, spiritualistic healings, and the like. I ask the Lord Jesus to remove all curses, spells, hexes, witchcraft spells, and voodoo spells, satanic spells, and occult evil, In the Name of Jesus. Heavenly Father, In the Name of Jesus and by the power of His shed Blood, I now renounce all expressions of anger, bitterness, rebellion and lack of submission to God's will exercised by persons who live on this property or in this home at the present or who previously lived here. I ask the Lord Jesus Christ to remove all anger, bitterness, rebellion, stubbornness, and spirits of separation seeking to rule this home. In the Name of Jesus Christ and by the power of His shed Blood, I now renounce all expressions of pride and control exercised by persons who live on this property or in this home at the present time or who previously lived here. I ask the Lord Jesus Christ to remove all prideful spirits and all controlling spirits.

In the Name and authority of Jesus Christ and by the power of His shed Blood, I now renounce all acts of immorality, impurity, indecency, strife, jealousy, selfishness, drunkenness, drug abuse, envy exercised by people (or a person) who live or lived on this property or in this home at the present or who previously lived here. I ask the Lord Jesus Christ to remove all immoral, impure, indecent, strifeful, jealous, selfish, drunkenness, drug abuse, and envious spirits. Heavenly Father, In the Name and authority of Jesus and by the power of His shed Blood, I now renounce all generational claims against this home and property including ground obtained through worship of false gods, practice of sorcery, fortune telling, consulting with mediums, freemasonry, or other secret organizations. I ask the Lord Jesus Christ to remove all demonic spirits associated with these wicked acts. Heavenly Father, I ask You to do these things according to John 14:14 in the Name of Jesus. Heavenly Father, I dedicate this home and property to You, it shall be a house of prayer, a house of praise and worship to You my Lord. In the Name of Jesus, I pray with thanksgiving. Amen.

Space for Journaling

Prayer of Deliverance

Heavenly Father, I repent of any sins in my life or my ancestors' lives that have resulted in a curse. I repent of all disobedience, rebellion, perversion, witchcraft, idolatry, lust, adultery, fornication, mistreatment of others, murder, cheating, lying, sorcery, divination, and occult involvement. I ask for Your forgiveness and cleansing through the blood of the Lord Jesus Christ.

I take authority over and break any and every curse upon my life in the Name of Jesus. I break all curses of poverty, lack, debt, destruction, sickness, death, and vagabondism. I break all curses on my marriage, family, children, and relationships. I break curses of rejection, pride, rebellion, lust, hurt, incest, rape, Ahab, Jezebel, fear, insanity, madness, and confusion.

I break all curses affecting my finances, mind, sexual character, emotions, will, and relationships.

I break every jinx, hex, spell and spoken curse over my life.

I break every fetter, shackle, chain, cord, habit, and cycle that is the result of a curse.

According to Galatians 3:13, I have been redeemed from *"the curse of the law"* by the sacrifice of Jesus. I exercise my faith in the blood of Jesus and loose my descendants and myself from any and every curse. I claim forgiveness through the blood of Jesus for the sins of the fathers.

All my sins have been remitted, and I loose myself from the curses that came as a result of all disobedience and rebellion to the Word of God.

I exercise my faith, and I know that confession is made unto salvation (Romans 10:10). Therefore, I confess that Abraham's blessings are mine (Galatians 3:14). I am not cursed, but blessed. I am *"the head, and not the tail*" (Deuteronomy 28:13). I am blessed coming in and blessed going out. I am blessed, and what God has blessed cannot be cursed.

I command spirits of rejection, hurt, bitterness, unforgiveness, bondage, torment, death, destruction, fear, lust, perversion, mind control, witchcraft, poverty, lack, debt, confusion, double-mindlessness, sickness, infirmity, pain, divorce, separation, loneliness, self-pity, self-destruction, self-rejection, anger, rage, wrath, anguish, vagabondism, abuse, and addiction to come out in the name of Jesus!

Lord, I thank you for setting me free from every curse and every spirit that has operated in my life as a result of a curse. Amen.[21]

Space for Journaling

Shattering Strongholds Prayer

Heavenly Father, In the Name and authority of Jesus Christ and by the power of His shed Blood, you are my battle-axe and my weapon of war. With you, O Lord, I shatter infirmities, sickness, disease and death.

With you, I shatter fear, rejection, pride, unbelief, doubt, bitterness, torment, anger, confusion and unforgiveness, jealous and envy.

With you, I shatter poverty, lack, debt and financial destruction.

With you, I shatter spiritual and physical abortions and miscarriages.

With you, I shatter abuse, lust, rape, and incest.

With you, I shatter spousal abuse, adultery, fornication, divorce and separation.

With you, I shatter compromise, laziness and slothfulness.

With you, I shatter addictions, perversions, obsessions, cravings and lust.

With you, I shatter chains, cords, shackles, spells, and curses over my life and my family.

With you, I shatter counterfeit shepherds and itching eared flocks.

With you, I shatter false prophets, false teachers, false anointing and temple harlots.

With you, I shatter the Spirit of Competition, the Spirit of Jezebel, the Spirit of Absalom, the Spirit of Ananias & Sapphira, the Spirit of Leviathan, the Spirit of Belial, the Spirit of Carnality, the Spirit of Fear, the Spirit of Compromise, the Spirit of Jealousy, the Spirit of Pride, and the Spirit of Anti-Christ that are infiltrating the church.

Declarative Prayers

With you, I shatter false anointing and release Your anointing to destroy the yokes of bondage.

With you, I shatter all chains, cords, shackles, spells, and curses over my church.

With you, I shatter corrupt city, state and federal governments and governmental officials.

With you, I shatter all chains, cords, shackles, spells, and curses over our city, state and federal government.

Through the Blood of Jesus, I loose myself, my family, my church, my city, my state and all governmental agencies from the bondages of the enemy and command the spirits that once controlled these areas back to the pits of hell, never to return. In the name of Jesus.

According to Galatians 3:13, I have been redeemed from *"the curse of the law"* by the sacrifice of Jesus. I exercise my faith in the power of the shed Blood of

Jesus, destroy every stronghold of the enemy, and loose myself from every curse.

Lord, I thank you for setting me free from every curse and every spirit that has operated in my life, church, and government. I thank you that we are free to love, obey and worship you.

We will be still, and know that You are God; You will be exalted among the nations, You will be exalted in the earth" (Psalm 46:10). In the Name of Jesus. Amen.

Cleansing Your Church or Ministry

Heavenly Father, I come to You now in the Name of my Lord and Savior, Jesus Christ. Father, in the Name and Authority of the Lord Jesus Christ and by the power of His Shed Blood, I (we) ask you to loose your angels into _____church or ministry name _____ and force out and drive out all foul, wicked, demon, tormenting, lying, hindering, seducing, perverse, familiar, unclean spirits, and demonic strongmen. I ask you Lord Jesus to send them back to the pits of hell, never to return to this church or ministry or any place on it's property.

I (we) now renounce all opportunities for ground held by Satan's wicked demons in relation to our church\ministry. I (we) bind with chains and fetters of iron all wicked spirits and their schemes and assignments, against this church\ministry. I (we) ask You Lord Jesus to evict them from this church\ministry, with any controlling powers of darkness, and to send them back to the pits of hell where they may never control or harm any person again. Heavenly Father, in the Name and authority of Jesus Christ and by the power of His shed Blood, I (we) now renounce all past use of this church\ministry for false religions, occult practices, divination, magic, sorcery, witchcraft, spiritualistic healings, and the like. I (we) ask the Lord Jesus to remove all curses, spells, hexes, witchcraft spells, voodoo spells, satanic spells, and occult evil, In the Name of Jesus. Heavenly Father, In the Name and authority of Jesus Christ and by the power of His shed Blood, I (we) now renounce all expressions of anger, bitterness, rebellion and lack of submission to God's will exercised by persons who have been on this property, preached or taught in this church\ministry at the present or who previously been here. I (we) ask the Lord Jesus Christ to remove all anger, bitterness, rebellion, stubbornness, and spirits of separation seeking to rule this church\ministry. Heavenly Father, In the Name and authority of Jesus Christ and by the power of His shed Blood, I (we) now renounce all expressions of pride and control exercised by persons who have been on this property, preached or taught in this church\ministry at the present or who previously been here. I (we) ask the Lord Jesus Christ to remove all prideful spirits and all controlling spirits and render them powerless, harmless and destroy the power of the enemy and any strongmen or demonic spirits over this church\ministry.

Heavenly Father, In the Name and authority of Jesus Christ and by the power of His shed Blood, I (we) now renounce all acts of immorality, impurity, indecency, strife, jealousy, selfishness, drunkenness, drug abuse, or envy exercised by people (or a person) who have been on this property, preached or taught in this church\ministry at the present or who previously been here. I (we) ask the Lord Jesus Christ to remove all immoral, impure, indecent, strifeful, jealous, selfish, drunkenness, drug abuse, and envious spirits. Heavenly Father, In the Name and authority of Jesus Christ and by the power of His shed Blood, I (we) now renounce all generational claims against this church\ministry and property including ground obtained through worship of false gods, practice of sorcery, fortune telling, consulting with mediums, freemasonry, or other secret organizations. I (we) ask the Lord Jesus Christ to remove all demonic spirits associated with these wicked acts. Heavenly Father, I (we) ask You to do these things according to John 14:14 in the Name of Jesus Christ. Heavenly Father, I (we) dedicate this church\ministry and property to You, it shall be a house of prayer, a house of praise and worship to You my (our) Lord. In the Name of Jesus I (we) pray with thanksgiving. Amen.

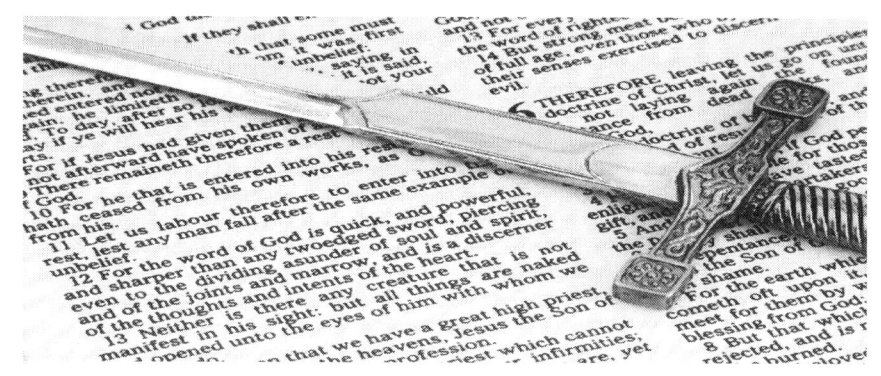

Appendix

Scripture on Spiritual Warfare

Demon List

12 Spirits Raging Against the Church

About the Author

Books and Materials by Dr. Jacquie

The Art of Spiritual Warfare

Scriptures for Spiritual Warfare

"And he said, Hearken ye, all Judah, and ye inhabitants of Jerusalem, and thou king Jehoshaphat, Thus saith the LORD unto you, Be not afraid nor dismayed by reason of this great multitude; for the battle is not yours, but God's."

(2 Chronicles 20:15)

You will not have to fight this battle. Take up your positions; stand firm and see the deliverance the LORD will give you, O Judah and Jerusalem. Do not be afraid; do not be discouraged. Go out to face them tomorrow, and the LORD will be with you' "

(2 Chronicles 20:17).

"But Moses said to the people, "Do not fear! Stand by and see the salvation of the LORD which He will accomplish for you today; for the Egyptians whom you have seen today, you will never see them again forever"

(Exodus 14:13).

"Now then, stand still and see this great thing the LORD is about to do before your eyes!"

(1 Samuel 12:16)

(For the weapons of our warfare are not carnal, but mighty through God to the pulling down of strong holds;) Casting down imaginations, and every high thing that exalteth itself against the knowledge of God, and bringing into captivity every thought to the obedience of Christ.

(2 Co 10:4-5)

He teacheth my hands to war, so that a bow of steel is broken by mine arms.

(Psalm 18:34)

Praise be to the LORD my Rock, who trains my hands for war, my fingers for battle.

(Psalm 144:1)

Every purpose is established by counsel: and with good advice make war.

(Proverbs 20:18)

Demon List

This book would not be complete without a list of demons you will encounter in spiritual warfare. The list includes:

1. The name of the demon spirit.
2. Subordinate spirits operating with them.
3. Effects or symptoms associated with it.
4. Bible scriptures to reference.

This is only a partial list, but I pray it helps you discern what spirits may be in operation against you, your family or your ministry. We must not be ignorant of Satan's devices or the spirits that are under his control. We must be equipped with the tools necessary to defeat the kingdom of darkness.

The Demon List

Spirit of **Absalom:** Pride, defiance, lying, rebellion, lust, murder, betrayal, treachery, power hungry, self-promotion. The Absalom spirit works against ministries\churches to destroy authority (2 Samuel 13:1-19).

Spirit of **Addiction:** Compulsion, dependence, obsession, craving, infatuation. Obsession with drugs, alcohol, food, cigarettes, sex or anything that causes a severe or uncontrollable need (Romans 13:14).

Spirit of **Affliction:** Suffering, difficulty, burden, problem, hardship, pain, trouble, misery, misfortune, illness, sickness, disease, disorder, complaint, infirmity, weakness (Psalm 34:19).

Spirit of **Adultery:** Infidelity, falseness, adultery, treachery, betrayal, deceitfulness, faithlessness (2 Peter 2:14; James 4:4). Adultery can spiritual or physical.

Spirit of **Ahab:** Anxiety, blind obedience, compromise, confusion, demonic slavery, worry, insecurity, manipulation, dependent on others, immoral (1 Kings 16:33; 18:17-18). Works in agreement with Jezebel spirit.

Spirit of **Ananias and Sapphira**: Lying, fraud, greed, manipulation, dishonesty, disrespect, deception (Acts 5:1-10).

Spirit of **Anti-Christ:** False miracles, defiance, division, hatred, perversion, pride, bondage. Religious spirit that functions to undermine and fight against Jesus Christ and the word of God (1 John 2:9; 18; 4:1-6).

Spirit of **Arrogance:** Haughtiness, egotism, pride, overconfidence, self-importance, condescension (2 Kings 14:10; Psalm 86:14; Proverbs 14:16; 2 Timothy 3:2).

Spirit of **Asherah**: Idolatry, lust (Exodus 34:13-15; 1 Kings 16:33; 2 Chronicles 14:3).

Spirit of **Baal:** Idolatry, Lust (Num. 25:3-5; 1 Kings 16:32; 1 Kings 18:19, 21, 22, 25, 26, 40; 19:18).

Spirit of **Babylon**: Frustration, sabotage, hindrances, imprisonment (Jeremiah 42:1-12; Luke 22:1-5; Revelation 16:8-17; 18:1-12).

Spirit of **Backlash:** Repercussion, counterattack, criticism, hostile response. There are demonic repercussions for those who attack and destroy Satan's kingdom agenda.

Spirit of **Beelzebub:** A ruling spirit (Matthew 12:24).

Spirit of **Belial:** Carnality, deception, wickedness, rebellion, witchcraft, lying, lust (Deut. 13:13; Judges 19:22-23; 2 Cor. 6:15).

Bewitching spirit: Casting of evil spell to bring a person under another's power or influence.

Spirit of **Bitterness:** Acrimony, unpleasantness, anger, animosity, hostility, cynicism, indignation, resentment (Hebrews 12:15; James 3:14).

Spirit of **Carnality**: Worldliness, lust, envy, indulgence, hedonism, decadence, sensuality, carnality (Numbers 11:4-5; 1 Cor. 3:3; 10:6-10).

Spirit of **Chemosh:** Moabite idol. Has two forms (1) **incubus:** spirit that attempts sexual intercourse with women. **Succubus:** spirit that attempts sexual intercourse with men (Num 25: 1-2).

Spirit of **Competition:** Ambition, contest, rivalry, pride, jealousy, resentment, opposition. The spirit of competition is raging through the church at an alarming rate (John 9:16; 10:19).

Spirit of **Compromise**: Settlement, arrangement, bargain, concession, give in, concede. When the Spirit of compromise infiltrates a church\ministry it lessens, decreases, weakens, diminishes the strength of the church in order to pacify the people.

Spirit of **Confusion:** perplexity, puzzlement, turmoil, uncertainty, mystification, lack of direction, disorganization. Keeps ministry from functioning in truth and Godly order (1 Corinthians 14:33; James 3:16).

Spirit of **Control**: Domination, manipulation, witchcraft. Associated with Jezebel spirit.

Spirit of **Delilah**: Lying, manipulation, seduction, sensuality, sexuality, treachery (Judges 16:4, 6, 10, 12, 13, 18).

Spirit of **Depression**: Despair, sadness, unhappiness, downheartedness, hopelessness, sleepiness, gloominess (Isaiah 61:3).

Diva spirit: A goddess or priestess of deities whose celebration of the idol included performances of a dramatic nature. The term comes from divination.

Spirit of **Divination:** Seeking knowledge by supernatural means, prediction, foretelling, insight, premonition, second sight (Jer. 14:14, Lev. 19:26; Acts 16:16). Divination is forbidden by God Deut. 18:10.

Spirit of **Doubt:** Hesitation, uncertainty, reservation, misgiving, distrust, disbelief, suspicion. Stops the flow of God working in you (Mt. 14:31; Mt. 21:21; James 1:6).

Familiar Spirits: Familiar with your family, can travel from generation to generation. Occurs in occult practices such as séances (1 Samuel 28:7).

Spirit of **Fear:** Terror, dread, anxiety, horror, distress, fright, panic, alarm, trepidation, worry, anxiety, phobia, overly shy, heaviness, Fear takes on many forms: fear of flying, fear of water, fear of people, fear of crowds, fear of change, fear of animals, and fear of heights (Psalm 91:5; 1 John 4:18; 2 Timothy 1:7).

Spirit of **Greed:** Gluttony, ravenousness, hunger, insatiability, self-indulgence, craving, lust, covetousness, materialism, acquisitiveness, longing, desire, selfishness (Ephesians 4:19).

Spirit of **Gossip:** Hearsay, scandal, blabbermouth, tattletale, rumormonger, bigmouth gossipmonger, scandalmonger (2 Cor. 12:20).

Spirit of **Haughtiness:** Proud, arrogant, conceited, self-important, superior, self-aggrandizing, high and mighty, condescending (Proverbs 18:12).

Spirit of **Incest:** Operates through curses of lust and perversion. (Lev. 20:12 NASB; 1 Cor. 5:5 AMP; 2 Cor. 2:5 AMP; 2 Cor. 7:11 AMP).

Spirit of **Jealousy:** Belittlement, envy, covetousness, resentment, pride, false entitlement, greed, obsession, manipulation, discord, possessiveness, insecurity (1 Samuel 18:5-11; Proverbs 3:31, 6:34; Ezekiel 8:1-12).

Spirit of **Jezebel:** Rebellion, witchcraft, control. Jezebel's objective is to destroy God's order in churches and families. Works with the Spirit of Ahab (1 Kings 18:21-25; 2 Kings 9:22).

Spirit of **Judas**: Betrayal, deception, disloyalty, lust, sabotage, traitor, treachery (Matthew 26:25).

Spirit of **Korah:** Arrogance, deceit, disrespect, rebellion against leadership (Numbers 16:1-19).

Spirit of **Lack:** Poverty, deprivation, shortage, never having enough (Nehemiah 5:1-11; Proverbs 11:24).

Legion: Army, troop, squad, multitude, host, team, crowd, group, throng, mass, gang, band (Mark 5:1-20).

Spirit of **Leviathan:** Arrogance, pride, conceit, destruction. Leviathan operates through a curse (Psalm 119:21; Proverbs 16:18).

Spirit of **Lust:** Envy, covetousness, longing, yearning, hunger, thirst, itch. Lust operates in many areas such as: sexual, abuse, adultery, rape, perversion, uncleanness (1 John 2:16).

Spirit of **Lying:** Dishonesty, deceit, duplicity, falseness, untruthfulness, insincerity, distrust, mendaciousness (1Kings 22:22-23 NIV).

Spirit of **Mammon:** Greed, materialism, ambition, love of money or the god of money (Matthew 6:24).

Spirit of **Manipulation:** Control, deception, lying, maneuvering, exploitation, persuasion, scheming. Can operate with Jezebel spirit.

Spirit of **Masturbation:** Self-abuse, lust, pornography, pleasuring oneself (Genesis 38:9).

Spirit of **Mental Illness:** Confusion, depression, delusions, derangement, insanity, paranoia, schizophrenia, worry (Mark 5:1-20).

Spirit of **Molech:** Abortion, sacrifice of children, murder (Leviticus 18:21; 20:2-5).

Spirit of **Molestation:** Abuse, rape, incest, violation, physically abused, battered, badly treated, injured, harmed, mistreated, maltreated, neglected, and molested.

Spirit of **Murder:** Kill, assassination, revenge, execute, massacre, slaughter, homicide, suicide, manslaughter, scandal, persecution. Murder can be physical, emotional or psychological (Psalm 10:8; Mathew 15:19; 1 John 3:15).

Spirit of **Obsession:** Fascination, fixation, passion, preoccupation, overly affectionate, domination. Control in any form: physical, mind, psychological. Obsession can occur with people, objects, and thoughts.

Spirit of the **Occult:** Opens the doors for multiple curses of death, destruction, sickness, disease. <u>Objects of the occult include</u>: Extra Sensory Perception (ESP), hypnosis, divination, necromancy, fortune telling, crystal balls, Ouija boards, tarot cards, séances, mediums, psychics, the New Age Movement, amulets and clairvoyance. <u>Other objects include</u>: occult movies, games, forms of bondage, books and music. <u>Forms of the occult</u>: Santeria, Wicca, Druids, Mysticism. <u>Occult practitioners</u>: shaman, healers, soothsayers, mediums, druids, magicians, sorcerer, necromancer, and occultist (1 Samuel 15:23; 2 Ch 33:6; Gal 5:20).

Spirit of **Oppression:** Heaviness, despair, depression, affliction, burdened, worried, troubled, overloaded, fraught, beset, beleaguered, plagued (Psalms 22:24; Proverbs 18:14). Works with spirit of depression.

Palmistry: Palm reading, fortune telling, divination, psychic power, second sight, extrasensory perception, sixth sense, telepathy, fortune telling, astrology, soothsaying, and occult practice.

Spirit of **Persecution:** Unfairness, condemnation, torment, annoyance, irritation, harassment. (Lamentation 5:5; Matt. 13:21; Romans 8:35).

Spirit of **Pride:** Arrogance, conceit, smugness, self-importance, egotism, vanity, immodesty, superiority. (2 Chronicles 32:26; Job 35:12; Ps. 10:2; 1 Timothy 3:6).

Spirit of **Rebellion:** disobedient, defiant, stubborn, pride, unmanageable, uncontrollable, self-will, selfishness, judgmental, (Deut. 31:27; 1 Samuel 15:23; Ezra 4:19; Proverbs 17:11).

Spirit of **Rejection:** Inferiority, inadequacy, self-condemnation, hopelessness, criticism, attention seeking, guilt, self-pity, low self-esteem. Rejection can open the door for other spirits: pride, rebellion, bitterness, insecurity, fear, offense, shame, intolerance, frustration, shyness (1 Sam 15:26; 16:1).

Spirit of **Religion:** Division, obsession with doctrines, denominationalism, false anointing, legalism, conservatism, mysticism. Religious spirits bring error, confusion, unbelief, heresy, pride, self-righteousness, and deception (Matt 23:17; Gal. 1:13-14; 1 Tim. 4:1-2).

Spirit of **Resentment:** Anger, bitterness, dislike, hatred, antipathy, offense. Operates with spirits of bitterness and unforgiveness.

Spirit of **Sabotage:** Disruption, damage, interruption, interference. Sabotage can be physical or spiritual through rebellion, destruction, deceitfulness or seditions (Neh. 2:10; 17-20; 4:1, 9, 13-14; 6:1-14).

Sanctimonious Spirit: holier-than-thou, smug, pious, pompous, superior, counterfeit holiness.

Spirit of **Seduction:** Deception, false religion, flattery, lying, false prophets, sensuality. Delilah or Jezebel spirits (1 Kings 11:1-8; 1 Timothy 4:1-6) (Delilah: Judges 16:4, 6, 10, 12, 13, and 18).

Spirit of **Selfishness:** Stinginess, self-life, self-indulgent.

Self-Righteous Spirit: smug, self-satisfied, complacent, pious, haughty, hypocritical, pompous, pretentious, and holier-than-thou.

Spirit of **Shame:** Anguish, disgrace, embarrassment, false humility, dishonor, humiliation, indignity, isolation, instability, victimization (Psalm 69:7).

Spirit of **Slavery:** Bondage, control. There are many forms of slavery: poverty, racism, lack, addiction, debt, sexual. Spirits of: Egypt, Pharaoh, Herod (Exodus 1:7-22; 3:7; Matthew 2:16).

Spirit of **Sodom and Gomorrah:** Perversion, homosexuality, hidden guile (Gen 18:20; 19:24; 19:28).

Soothsaying: False prophecy, zodiacal, prediction, horoscopic, fortune-telling, stargazing, foretelling forecasting, prognosis, divination, projection, foreseeing (See also occult) (Leviticus 19:26).

Soul Ties: Friendships that are false, manipulation, deception, spiritual blindness. Can enter in through unhealthy relationships, sexual relationships such as adultery, premarital sex. Also a form of witchcraft.

Spirit of **Stinginess:** Cheap, miserliness, parsimony, meanness, tightfistedness (2 Corinthians 9:7).

Strongholds: Fortress, bastion, citadel, fort, castle. Spiritual strongholds such as pride, rebellion, stubbornness, slavery, religious spirit are mental strongholds (2 Corinthians 10:4-5).

Spirit of **Strongman**: A ruling spirit based on Matthew 12:29. The strongman can be fear, un-forgiveness, bitterness, lust, pride, anger, infirmity, rebellion. Acts as a gatekeeper for demonic influence to come in.

Spirit of **Suicide:** Perversity, morbid, forlorn, irresponsibility, madness, self-destruction, desperate, cheerless, hopeless, miserable.

Spirit of **Tamar:** Whoredom, manipulation, temptress (Genesis 38:24).

Third Eye: Witchcraft or second sight. Divinators use it to see into the spirit realm.

Spirit of **Unbelief:** Doubt, non-belief, skepticism, incredulity, agnosticism, atheism, faithless, distrust.

Uncleanness: Filthiness, impurity, squalor, unsanitary, sinfulness, impurity, unworthiness, unseemliness, immoral, tainted, foul (Luke 4:33 and Mark 9:25).

Unteachable Spirit**:** Disinclined, ill disposed, unwilling, defensive, intolerant, and rigid. Refuses to accept teachings from leadership in the church.

Spirit of the **Vagabond:** Vagrant, drifter, beggar, hobo, traveler, wanderer, gypsy, nomad. There are individuals in the church that are spiritual vagabonds wandering from church to church never finding a home.

Vain Imagination: Useless thoughts or dead end thinking (2 Corinthians 10:4-5).

Voodoo: Conjure up, curse, spell, jinx, enchantment, supernatural, sorcery, witchcraft, augury, alchemy, deviltry, incantation, conjuring, tricks, trickery, illusion, sleight of hand, artifice, charm, trick, spellbind.

Spirit of Witchcraft: Spirits operating outside of Godly realm. Witchcraft is rebellion against God. Cults and religions such as Wicca, New Age, and Transcendental Meditation or TM engage in some form of witchcraft practices.

Spirit of **Whoredom:** Lustful spirit, seductive spirit, uncleanness, lasciviousness, idolatry, sexuality (Jeremiah 3:9; Hosea 1:2).

Wild Spirit: Foolish, unconventional, irrational, reckless, madcap, messy, undisciplined, riotous, unruly, rough, unmanageable, uncontrollable, disorderly.

Spirit of **Worry:** Apprehension, anxiety, fear, care, burden, anxiety, uneasiness, disquiet, discomfort, apprehension, nervousness.

12 Spirits Raging Against the Church

During prayer, the Lord spoke to me regarding spirits that are raging against the church. He said that the following spirits are rampant in the church due to the lack of spiritual warfare.

The list below outlines the twelve spirits that are attacking the church. Believers are being spiritually beheaded while sitting in the building as the battle makes them weary and they begin to loose ground.

1. **Spirit of Competition** (John 9:16; 10:19)
2. **Spirit of Jezebel** (1 Kings 18:21-25; 2 Kings 9:22; Revelation 2:20)
3. **Spirit of Absalom** (2 Samuel 13:1-19)
4. **Spirit of Ananias & Sapphira** (Acts 5:1-10)
5. **Spirit of Leviathan** (Ps. 119:21; Pro. 16:18)
6. **Spirit of Belial** (Deut. 13:13; Judges 9:22-23; 2 Cor. 6:15)

7. **Spirit of Carnality** (Num. 11:4-5; 1 Cor. 3:3; 10:6-10)

8. **Spirit of Fear** (Ps. 91:5; 2 Timothy 1:7)

9. **Spirit of Compromise** (Rev 2:20-21)

10. **Spirit of Jealousy** (1 Samuel 18:5-11; Pro. 3:31; 6:34; Ez. 8:1-12

11. **Spirit of Pride** (2 Chron 32:26; Ps 10:2; Job 35:12; 1 Timothy 3:6)

12. **Spirit of Anti-Christ** (1 John 2:9; 4:1-6; 1 John 2:18; 22)

The Church in the Age to Come

When you look at the church as it enters the final chapter in the war against it, you will begin to see the church in the same manner as the Apostle John in The Book of Revelation. As we turn the page and see the modern day church shifts its focus from a Christ driven church to secular humanistic church, we can see a pattern that emulates the seven churches. Are we headed on a downward course toward a Laodicean lukewarm state?

- **Religious\Left First Love:** The church in Ephesus: Revelation 2:1-6.

- **Persecuted**: The church in Smyrna: Revelation 2:8-10.

- **Compromising/Worldliness:** The church in Pergamum: Revelation 2:12-16.

- **Jezebel:** The church in Thyatira: Revelation 2:18-28.

- **Dead\Traditional:** The church in Sardis: Revelation 3:3-5.

- **Weak\Persevering**: The church in Philadelphia: Revelation 3:7-12.

- **Lukewarm\Prideful:** The church in Laodicea: Revelation 3:14-21.

As believers, we must pray against all spirits that come against the church and we must be watchful of the portals and gateways we leave open for their attack. The Lord also said that in this season, the enemy dispatched powerful demons against us. Demons unlike any we have ever encountered. Therefore, we must increase our prayer, fasting and intercession within the church. We must be the watchmen on the wall. Jude 1:4 gives us this warning, "For there are certain men crept in unawares, who were before of old ordained to this condemnation, ungodly men, turning the grace of our God into lasciviousness, and denying the only Lord God, and our Lord Jesus Christ." We are also told in 1 John 4:1-3 "Beloved, believe not every spirit, but try the spirits whether they are of God: because many false prophets are gone out into the world. Hereby know ye the Spirit of God: Every spirit that confesseth that Jesus Christ is come in the flesh is of God: And every spirit that confesseth not that Jesus Christ is come in the flesh is not of God: and this is that spirit of antichrist, whereof ye have heard that it should come; and even now already is it in the world."

Finally, we are given this warning concerning the anti-Christ: "Little children, it is the last time: and as ye have heard that antichrist shall come, even now are there many antichrists; whereby we know that it is the last time" (1 John 2:18). "Who is a liar but he that denieth that Jesus is the Christ? He is antichrist, that denieth the Father and the Son" (1 John 2:22).

Do you know the depths of Satan? Do you know the depths that he will go to destroy us, the church and everything that represents the True and Living God? Jesus warns and assures us that if we endure to the end, He will reward us: "But unto you I say…as many as have not this doctrine, and which have not known the depths of Satan, as they speak; I will put upon you none other burden. But that which ye have already hold fast till I come. And he that overcometh, and keepeth my works unto the end, to him will I give power over the nations: And he shall rule them with a rod of iron; as the vessels of a potter shall they be broken to shivers: even as I received of my Father. And I will give him the morning star. He that hath an ear, let him hear what the Spirit saith unto the churches" (Revelation 2:24-29).

Therefore, having done ALL, Stand, undaunted, unmovable, unshakeable and uncompromising on the word of God.

About the Author

God has called Dr. Jacquie Hadnot to encourage, inspire, motivate and activate the gifts of the Spirit in order to raise powerful ministries in the body of Christ. She is becoming a voice on the subject of prayer, worship and spiritual warfare.

She is recognized as a modern-day apostle with a strong prophetic and psalmist anointing. She has a revelational teaching ministry with a mandate to saturate the world with the Word of God. Jacquie's heart is to see people arise and walk in the destiny and inheritance of the Lord.

She has founded and established It Is Written Ministries, a publication company, an accounting and consulting firm, and a global radio station. As a retired accountant and financial executive, Jacquie blends ministerial and entrepreneurial applications in her ministry to enrich and empower a diverse audience with skills and abilities to take kingdoms for the Lord Jesus Christ. A lecturer, conference speaker, teacher, business trainer, and financial consultant, she provides consulting services to businesses, churches, and individuals. She has written over twenty-five books, manuals, and other materials on intimacy with God, prayer, fasting and spiritual warfare. She has also released several music Cds and received numerous music, book and community service awards. She also received the ABMA Image Award for worldwide evangelism.

Beyond the pulpit, Jacquie is a talk-show host on both television and radio with her own program, Light for Your Path. Weekly she applies God's wisdom to today's world solutions. Her ministry goal is to make Christ's teachings relevant for today. She also publishes a quarterly magazine by the same name.

In addition to her vast experience, Jacquie has a Th.d. in Pastoral Theology and an M.min. in Ministry Leadership. She is also a wife, mother of one daughter and grandmother of one grandson. She and her husband, Gregory presently pastor It Is Written Ministries in Kansas City Kansas. They also serve as owners and corporate officers of Igniting the Fire Media Group.

Other Books & Materials by Dr. Jacquie

Books in Print
- Closing the Doors to Satan's Attacks: *Overcoming Fear*
- Trapped in the Arms of Death: *Overcoming Grip of Suicide*
- The Extravagant Love of God: Experiencing the Prophetic Flow
- Cry Aloud, Spare Not! A Prophetic Call to the Fast God Has Chosen
- Cry Aloud, Spare Not! The Companion-Study Guide
- His Mercy Endures Forever: Psalms, Prayers & Meditations
- To Make War with the Saints; Satan's Kingdom Agenda
- A Treasure in the Pleasure of Loving God
- Loving God through His Names: 365 Days of the Year
- Where Is Your God? Have We Lost the Referential Fear of the Lord?

Booklets
- When Fear Crept In
- Deeper…
- Naked, Broken and Unashamed

Audio Books & Teachings
- More of You… (Volume 1)
- In the Face of Adversity: *Overcoming Life's Storms*
- Be Not Deceived…
- Where Is Your God?
- Recognizing Your Due Season
- Praying the Healing Scriptures
- The Enemy in Me: *Overcoming Self-Life Issues*

The Art of Spiritual Warfare

- ➤ Trusting God in a Season of Discouragement
- ➤ The Harlot Heart

Music
- ➤ The Extravagant Love of God
- ➤ The Spoken Word of Love
- ➤ His Mercy Endures Forever: Praying the Psalms

DVD
- ➤ When Your Faith is Being Tested
- ➤ What Made David Run
- ➤ Agents of Change
- ➤ Virtuous Women of Worship

Recommended Reading

Strongman: His NAME? What's His Game?
Drs. Jerry & Carol Robeson

To Make War with the Saints: Satan's Kingdom Agenda
Dr. Jacquelyn Hadnot

Warfare of the Spirit
A.W. Tozer

Identifying and Breaking Curses
John Eckhardt

Training the Prophets
Dr. Margaret Wright

E.M. Bounds
Guide to Spiritual Warfare

TO CONTACE DR. JACQUIE:

www.jacquiehadnot.com
www.ignitingthefire.net
Or write us:
jacquie@jacquiehadnot.com

Notes

[1] C. Peter Wagner, Warfare Prayer (Regal Books, Ventura, CA 1991) pp. 16-18
[2] Encarta ® World English Dictionary © & (P) 1998-2005 Microsoft Corporation.
[3] Encarta ® World English Dictionary © & (P) 1998-2005 Microsoft Corporation.
[4] practical spiritual warfare.com May, 2009
[5] E.M. Bounds, Winning the Invisible War (Whitaker House, 1984), pp. 24
[6] The five virtues of humanity, righteousness, propriety, wisdom and faith are known as the Way.
[7] Encarta ® World English Dictionary © & (P) 1998-2005 Microsoft Corporation.
[8] Encarta ® World English Dictionary © & (P) 1998-2005 Microsoft Corporation.
[9] A.W. Tozer, Warfare of the Spirit. (Christian Publication 1993) pp 3, 4.
[10] Prayers,
[11] Isaiah 25:4, KJV.
[12] Timothy Paul Jones, (The Armor of God, Rose Publishing) 2008
[13] J.B Campbell, Sr., "Armies, Roman," in Oxford Classical Dictionary 3d ed., ed. Simon Hornblower and Anthony Spawforth (New York: Oxford University Press 1996) 172-173
[14] Timothy Paul Jones, The Armor of God, Rose Publishing 2008
[15] Timothy Paul Jones, The Armor of God, Rose Publishing 2008
[16] Timothy Paul Jones, The Armor of God, Rose Publishing 2008
[17] Timothy Paul Jones, The Armor of God, Rose Publishing 2008
[18] Timothy Paul Jones, The Armor of God, Rose Publishing 2008
[19] The Dake Annotated Reference Bible, pp 371.
[20] Soldiers Call, Bobbie Saulsberry.
[21] John Eckhardt, Identifying and Breaking Curses (Whitaker House 1999) pp.48.

Books & Reference Materials

Books and reference materials studied in preparation for the book.

The Art of War, the Ancient Classic
Published by: Capstone Publishing, West Sussex, United Kingdom

The Prophet's Dictionary
Dr. Paula Price
Published by: Whitaker House, New Kensington, PA

The Layman's Bible Dictionary
George W. Knight and Rayburn W. Kay
Published by: Barbour Books, Uhrichsville, OH

Encarta World English Dictionary
Microsoft Corporation

Practicalspiritualwarfare.com

Prayer of Salvation

No matter what you do in life, nothing else will matter except your relationship with Jesus Christ. A committed relationship with Jesus is the key to a victorious life. Our Lord and Savior laid down His life for us. He rose again for us so that we could spend eternity with Him. Jesus said, *"I am come that they might have life, and that they might have it more abundantly."*

It is God's will that everyone receive eternal salvation. The only way to receive salvation is to call upon the name of Jesus and confess Him as Lord of your life. The Bible says in Romans 10: 9-13, that if thou shalt confess with thy mouth the Lord Jesus, and shalt believe in thine heart that God hath raised him from the dead, thou shalt be saved. *For with the heart man believeth unto righteousness; and with the mouth, confession is made unto salvation. For the scripture saith, whosoever believeth on him shall not be ashamed. For there is no difference between the Jew and the Greek: for the same*

Lord over all is rich unto all that call upon him. For whosoever shall call upon the name of the Lord shall be saved.

God loves you, no matter who you are, no matter what your past. God loves you so much that He gave His one and only begotten Son for you. The Bible tells us *"...whoever believes in him shall not perish but have eternal life"* (John 3:16 NIV). Jesus laid down His life and rose again so that we could spend eternity with Him in heaven and experience His absolute best on earth. If you would like to receive Jesus into your life, say the following prayer aloud. It is vital that you mean it from your heart.

> *Heavenly Father, I come to You admitting that I am a sinner. Right now, I choose to turn away from sin, and I ask You to cleanse me of all unrighteousness. I believe that Your Son, Jesus, died on the cross to take away my sins. I also believe that He rose again from the dead so that I may be justified and made righteous through faith in Him. I call upon the name*

of Jesus Christ to be the Savior of my life. Jesus, I choose to follow You, and I ask that You fill me with the power of the Holy Spirit. I declare right now that I am a born-again child of God. I am free from sin, and full of the righteousness of God. I am saved in Jesus' name. Amen.

If you prayed this prayer to receive Jesus Christ as your Lord and Savior or if this book has blessed your life, we would like to hear from you. Please write us:

Igniting the Fire Publishing
1314 North 38th Street, Suite 101
Kansas City, KS 66102
Or
It Is Written Ministries
1314 North 38th Street, Suite 102
Kansas City, KS 66102

The Art of Spiritual Warfare

Made in the USA
Charleston, SC
30 May 2012